As the enraptured Ichabod fancied all this, and as he rolled his great green eyes over the fat meadowlands, the rich fields of wheat, of rye, of buckwheat, and Indian corn, and the orchards burdened with ruddy fruit, which surrounded the warm tenement of Van Tassel, his heart yearned after the damsel who was to inherit these domains, and his imagination expanded with the idea, how they might be readily turned into cash, and the money invested in immense tracts of wild land, and shingle palaces in the wilderness.

From "The Legend of Sleepy Hollow"
by Washington Irving

Love's a Mystery

Love's a Mystery in Sleepy Hollow, New York

Love's a Mystery

in Sleepy Hollow NY

Gabrielle Meyer &
Ruth Logan Herne

Love's a Mystery is a trademark of Guideposts.

Published by Guideposts Books & Inspirational Media
100 Reserve Road, Suite E200
Danbury, CT 06810
Guideposts.org

Copyright © 2022 by Guideposts. All rights reserved.

This book, or parts thereof, may not be reproduced, stored in a retrieval system, or transmitted in any form or by any means, electronic, mechanical, photocopying, recording, or otherwise, without the written permission of the publisher.

This is a work of fiction. While the setting of Love's a Mystery as presented in this series is fictional, the locations actually exist, and some places and characters may be based on actual places and people whose identities have been used with permission or fictionalized to protect their privacy. Apart from the actual people, events, and locales that figure into the fiction narrative, all other names, characters, businesses, and events are the creation of the author's imagination and any resemblance to actual persons or events is coincidental.

Every attempt has been made to credit the sources of copyrighted material used in this book. If any such acknowledgment has been inadvertently omitted or miscredited, receipt of such information would be appreciated.

Scripture references are from the following sources: *The Holy Bible, King James Version* (KJV). *The Holy Bible, New International Version* (NIV). Copyright ©1973, 1978, 1984, 2011 by Biblica, Inc. Used by permission of Zondervan. All rights reserved worldwide. www.zondervan.com

Cover and interior design by Müllerhaus
Cover illustration by Dan Burr, represented by Illustration Online LLC.
Typeset by Aptara, Inc.

Printed and bound in the United States of America
10 9 8 7 6 5 4 3 2 1

Love Learns the Truth

by
Gabrielle Meyer

I profess not to know how women's hearts are wooed and won. To me they have always been matters of riddle and admiration. Some seem to have but one vulnerable point, or door of access; while others have a thousand avenues, and may be captured in a thousand different ways. It is a great triumph of skill to gain the former, but a still greater proof of generalship to maintain possession of the latter, for a man must battle for his fortress at every door and window. He who wins a thousand common hearts is therefore entitled to some renown; but he who keeps undisputed sway over the heart of a coquette, is indeed a hero.

From "The Legend of Sleepy Hollow"
by Washington Irving

Chapter One

Sleepy Hollow, New York
Autumn, 1820

Deep purple, red, and orange blanketed the hills along the Hudson River. October had unfurled her brilliant colors across North Tarrytown, New York, which Hannie Van Brunt knew better as Sleepy Hollow. Fall was her favorite time of year, when the bountiful crops were harvested. The cooler air was redolent with the scent of woodsmoke and rain, and the farmers of Sleepy Hollow slowed their work to enjoy more visiting.

Hannie stood at the kitchen window, a mixing bowl in hand, as she admired the view. Her gaze surveyed the lane leading up to the old Van Tassel farm, waiting impatiently for her father's arrival. The farm was still known as the Van Tassel place, though her father, Abraham (or Brom, as he was known) Van Brunt, had inherited it upon his marriage to Hannie's mother, Katrina Van Tassel, thirty years ago that spring. Though it had been in the Van Tassel family for several generations, and they had enjoyed great prosperity, under her father's care it had flourished even more. It was widely known as the largest and prettiest farm in all of New York state—and it would be Hannie's one day—if, and only if, she married.

"There's no time to be woolgathering, child," Mama said as she bustled into the kitchen, her basket laden with vegetables from the kitchen garden. At the age of forty-nine, she was still as fair and beautiful as she was the day she married, or so Papa often told her. Mama always blushed and reminded him of her thickening middle or the silver hairs entwined amongst the golden strands, but Papa would pull her into his arms and tell her she only grew lovelier with age. "They'll be here any minute, and we've yet to get the *boterkoek* in the oven."

"I'm about to pour it into the pan now," Hannie said calmly as she spooned the butter cake batter into the prepared baking dish.

Salome, one of the well-paid house servants who often worked in the kitchen with Hannie, took the vegetables from Mama. She would stew the tomatoes for tomorrow's breakfast.

Mama went to the cast-iron stove and stirred the *boerenkaassoep*, a thick, vegetable cheese soup made from the *boerenkaas* Mama was known for across the hollow. It was an old family recipe, brought to the new world by Mama's ancestors from Holland. "Do you have the bread sliced and ready to fry?" she asked.

Hannie slipped the cake batter into the oven and then closed the door before lifting the cutting board and handing it to her mother. "We also sliced the cheese to melt onto the bread."

The kitchen was warm, but Mama seemed overly hot as she wiped her apron across her forehead. "I just want him to like us."

Placing her hand on her mother's shoulder, Hannie gave her a gentle squeeze. "You're the best cook in the county," she reassured her, "and you've made enough food to feed everyone in the hollow. I don't see how he could not be impressed."

Mama grabbed a pan and placed it next to the pot of soup. It wasn't like her to be so distracted or insecure, especially where her cooking was concerned.

It made Hannie pause for the first time since she learned that Mr. Gideon Webb would be boarding with them. "Mama?"

"Hmm?" she asked as she scooped lard into the pan. The little glob melted as it slid across the surface of the hot metal.

"Why are you so nervous about impressing the new schoolmaster?"

"Am I nervous?" Mama giggled uncomfortably.

Hannie crossed her arms over the high-waisted dress she wore. It was her second-best gown, with a dark green background and little pink flowers. It was now covered with an apron to keep it from getting soiled. She'd gone up to change earlier, knowing Mr. Webb would arrive while they were still preparing supper. She wanted to be ready to receive him.

"Is the table set?" Mama asked as she laid pieces of bread onto the melted lard.

"It's been set for hours."

"And you found some fresh flowers for the vases?"

"I placed a large bouquet of purple and white asters on the table." Hannie didn't move, though there was much to be done. "Who is Mr. Webb, Mama?"

"Hmm?" Mama seemed absentminded—very unlike her.

"I said…" Hannie moved into her mother's line of sight. "Who is Mr. Webb? And why are you so concerned about impressing him?"

Mama looked at Salome uncomfortably before she addressed Hannie. "He's the new schoolmaster, of course. You know that."

"What else is he?"

"Really, Hannie. You act as if I'm hiding something."

"I'll find out eventually. You might as well be up front with me."

Mama was never one to keep a secret long. Secrets felt like lies to her and she was too good and too kind to put up a strong defense.

"Oh, all right, if you must know." Mama let out a sigh and finally turned to Hannie, speaking quietly, though Salome had been with them for years and wasn't prone to gossip. "He's the son of a very good friend of mine from Springfield, Massachusetts. His father was a vicar, and his mother, my childhood friend, died when he was very young. When he sent his letter to inquire about the teaching position, I recognized his name and sent a letter to his father."

"And?" The Van Brunts were widely known for their hospitality and generosity. Why one more visitor would bring such anxiety to her mother was a mystery.

"And…" Mama paused as she flipped the fried bread over, revealing a perfectly golden top. "His father and your father exchanged—how should I say this—mutual interest in seeing the two of you paired."

"Paired?" Hannie's arms fell to her sides as Salome glanced over her shoulder in surprise. "As in, an arranged marriage?"

"Oh no." Mama laughed as she patted Hannie's arm. "Nothing as archaic as that, sweetheart. You know how concerned Papa and I are about your future happiness."

"You mean the future of the farm, don't you?" Hannie tried not to bristle, knowing her mother meant well, but also knowing that if she did not marry, the farm would be inherited by one of the Van Tassel cousins. Casper was next in line, though he was a lazy sort of fellow with a penchant for ale. He'd been eyeing the farm since he was a lad. Hannie knew that if he inherited the farm, he would squander all her father's hard work.

Yet, what was Hannie to do? Not one of the men in the hollow had ever turned her head—not seriously. They were either too arrogant, with little heart, or too spineless, with little brawn. She didn't know what she was looking for, but she knew she hadn't found it. At the age of twenty-four, she was beyond her prime and an old maid in the eyes of many neighbors and family members. But she refused to settle—even if that put the farm at risk.

"Your happiness is all that your father and I desire," Mama said, trying to reassure her.

"I will not find it in the arms of a stranger from Massachusetts," Hannie protested. "And a schoolmaster, at that! You of all people should know how distasteful a schoolmaster can be."

"Oh, hush," Mama said to Hannie. "I never took that awkward young man seriously. Mr. Irving's account was purely fiction."

She was referring to Mr. Ichabod Crane and the popular tale that the author Washington Irving had written and recently published. Mr. Irving had been to the hollow on several occasions and heard Papa spinning a tale about how he won the fair hand of Katrina Van Tassel from the schoolmaster, Mr. Ichabod Crane. Mr. Irving had been so enamored with Papa's storytelling, he'd included it in his serial collection of short stories and essays, which he'd entitled *The Sketch Book of Geoffrey Crayon, Gent*. The past year had brought much attention to Mama and Papa, though everyone in the hollow was familiar with the old story. Papa claimed it was all true, though Mama said he had embellished most of it.

Hannie didn't know fact from fiction where Ichabod Crane was concerned.

"I hope Papa didn't make any promises to the vicar," she said.

"Just a mutual desire to see our children happy and settled." Mama laid the sliced cheese on the fried bread to melt. "Mr. Webb is almost thirty, and he's spent the past ten years traveling the country. He's from a good and respectable family, but his father worries that he has not put down any roots. It is his hope that Mr. Webb will find a place to establish himself here in North Tarrytown."

"At the expense of my hand in marriage?"

"No promises were made," Mama said, her voice lowering a bit. "But now you know what your father hopes. Just keep an open mind, Hannie. That's all we ask."

A noise outside on the road brought all three of their heads up to look out the window. Papa's carriage came into view, pulled by two of the finest matching bay geldings in the county.

"They're here." Mama scooped the bread from the pan and placed it on a serving platter. "Get the soup dished up and out on the table, Hannie. Quick. Salome, make sure to take the cake out of the oven when it's finished baking. I want everything to be perfect."

"Yes, ma'am," Salome said.

Hannie did as her mother instructed, having helped at her mother's side as long as she could remember. She had learned everything her mother knew about cooking, baking, weaving, cheese-making, preserving, mending, sewing, managing the workers, and all the other odds and ends that came with running a large farm. Hannie had been trained to become the lady of the house, though whether she would ever take on that honor had yet to be seen.

She hurried with the finishing touches, her skirts swishing about her ankles as she worked, wishing Papa hadn't driven around the side of the house and out of sight. Though she had no intention of marrying Mr. Webb—or anyone else—she still couldn't quell the curiosity now burning within her. Would Papa press her to court Mr. Webb? Had Mr. Webb come to Sleepy Hollow with the intention of wooing her? Did he know that she came with a vast farm and a wealthy purse? The very thought that any man would want her for her money made her shudder.

"Off with your apron," Mama said as they completed their preparations, leaving the rest to Salome's capable hands. "And tuck your flyaway hairs into your cap. We wouldn't want Mr. Webb to see us—"

"As we truly are?" Hannie supplied.

"Oh, Hannie," Mama said with a chuckle. "Don't dismiss Mr. Webb without getting to know him first. That's all we're asking." She paused. "I think I hear them entering the house."

"Katrina," Papa called, "we're home."

Mama's blue eyes widened, and she grinned. "Let's go."

As Mama pushed through the swinging door, which led through a connecting hall and into the dining room, Hannie schooled her features and let out a sigh.

Mr. Webb would only be boarding with them for one week. After that, he would move on to the next family in the district. She could manage to fend him off for one week, couldn't she?

LOVE'S A MYSTERY

The Van Tassel mansion was even grander than Gideon had imagined. As he followed Mr. Van Brunt through the spacious rooms, smelling the tantalizing food, he was still amazed that he had finally met the real Brom Bones of Sleepy Hollow fame. Gideon's copy of *The Sketch Book* was tucked safely into his traveling bag, and he had read "The Legend of Sleepy Hollow" so many times, he practically had it memorized. He'd never been awestruck before meeting Brom, but his tongue had been tied since he'd stepped into the Van Brunts' handsome carriage. Perhaps it was Gideon's admiration for the legendary man—or the fact that Brom hadn't stopped talking since they'd met. His deep, baritone voice had kept Gideon enthralled all the way up the hills to the farm.

Gideon was a tall, muscular man, but he still felt shadowed next to Brom Bones. Whether in truth, or in his imagination, Gideon had not yet deciphered.

"I think you'll be quite pleased with Mrs. Van Brunt's cooking," Brom said, his barrel chest puffing out with pride. "She has taught our daughter, Hannie, everything she knows. Hannie will make a good wife."

"Is she engaged to be married?" Gideon asked, trying desperately to relax with his host. He would be in their home for a week. Surely, he wouldn't be tongue-tied the whole time.

Brom looked sharply at Gideon, studying him intently, making Gideon stand up a little straighter.

"Have you not spoken with your father?" Brom asked Gideon, surprising him with the change in topic.

"My father?" Gideon frowned. "Not for many months, I'm afraid."

Brom lifted his chin, as if this bit of information was important to him in some way.

"Katrina," Brom called out again, "we're home."

The dining room table was laden with beautiful china, silver, and crystal. At least a dozen dishes were laid out, awaiting consumption. Steam spiraled off golden sweet corn dripping with butter, spinach coated in cream sauce, and stewed cranberries. There were other things, under covers, that teased his senses, causing his stomach to growl.

"Mr. Irving's descriptions of the food offerings at this fine table were not elaborated," Gideon found himself saying.

"You've read the story, then?" Brom asked as he indicated one of the chairs while he took a seat at the head of the table.

The kitchen door swung open at that moment, and Gideon rose from his seat at the sight of the famous Katrina Van Tassel—or rather, Mrs. Van Brunt, though she did not look old enough to be the heroine of Mr. Irving's tale.

"Ah," Brom said as he also rose. "Mr. Webb, this is my wife, Mrs. Van Brunt."

"It's a pleasure to meet you, Mr. Webb," Katrina said with a slight curtsy. Her clothing harkened back to a bygone era, influenced by her Dutch ancestry. She eyed him as closely as Brom had done just moments before. "And how is your father?"

Gideon couldn't hide his surprise. "Do you know my father, ma'am?"

"Yes—didn't you know? Your mother and I were old friends. I thought you knew that."

He shook his head. "I had no idea. What a wonderful surprise." All this time, he hadn't known there was a connection between his family and the well-known Van Brunts. Gideon's mother had died when he was still a baby, and his father hadn't spoken much about her life before they'd married.

Katrina looked to Brom, a question in her eyes.

"Mr. Webb," Brom said, "we'd like you to meet our daughter, Hannie."

Gideon had been so preoccupied meeting Katrina, he hadn't even looked at their daughter. When he turned to acknowledge her, his breath caught. Until he'd met Brom at the stagecoach stop just thirty minutes before, he hadn't even known the Van Brunts had a child—let alone such a beautiful daughter. She was exactly as Gideon had imagined the fair Katrina to look in "The Legend of Sleepy Hollow." Thick blond hair, tucked under a cap, though her curls tried to break loose as they teased her cheeks. Brilliant blue eyes, as wide as the Hudson River just beyond the Van Tassel farm. And features as delicate as they were striking. She wore a pretty green gown, a little old-fashioned, though more up-to-date than her mother's, and well made. Her cheeks were pink, whether from the heat of the kitchen, or their introduction, he couldn't tell.

She offered him an elegant curtsy. "How do you do, Mr. Webb?"

If he thought himself tongue-tied before, it was worse with Hannie Van Brunt gazing at him under the curtain of her thick eyelashes. Gideon prided himself on his confidence and self-assurance—but at the moment, he didn't feel like himself at all.

Finally, he bowed. "How do you do, Miss Van Brunt?"

There was an awkward hush while Brom and Katrina looked on, something hopeful gleaming from their gazes as they glanced between Gideon and Hannie.

"Shall we eat?" Katrina asked, indicating the table. "Have a seat, Mr. Webb."

"Please," he said, "if you were my mother's friend, you must call me Gideon."

That seemed to please Katrina a great deal. "How lovely. Won't you sit down, Gideon?"

He and Brom took their seats after Katrina and Hannie.

"Hannie made the boerenkaassoep," Katrina said. "It's an old family recipe, simple but hearty and delicious. We hope you'll enjoy it."

After everyone was settled, Brom said a prayer, and they began to eat.

The soup smelled delicious and was a feast for his eyes. It was full of several types of vegetables and bacon in a cheesy broth. He was offered fried sourdough bread with yellow cheese melted on the top, and when he saw the others dipping their bread into the soup, he did likewise.

It was the tastiest thing he'd ever eaten.

When he glanced up, he found three sets of eyes on him, and he knew they were waiting for his praise—which he heartily gave. "This is the best soup I've ever had."

Katrina and Brom grinned, though Hannie did not smile. Instead, she looked back at her own bowl and continued to eat.

Gideon wondered at her behavior. It was as if he had insulted her, though all he'd done was meet her.

"I'm surprised you did not hear from your father," Brom said to Gideon. "I wrote to him twice since we learned you were coming to North Tarrytown and received two of his letters in reply. Did he not take the time to write to you?"

"I was traveling this past month," Gideon said. "Not all of my mail has caught up to me, as yet."

"Ah." Brom nodded his understanding. "Perhaps when you receive his letter, you and I will have much to discuss."

Hannie's gaze snapped to her father, while Katrina blushed and Brom beamed.

Gideon had the distinct feeling he was missing something important. "Perhaps we will," he said with a noncommittal smile.

"What brings you to Sleepy Hollow?" Hannie finally spoke up, looking at him intently, as if he was guilty of something. "If not to rekindle a relationship with your mother's old friend?"

"I had no idea a relationship existed before now," he said, trying to sound civil, though he felt he was on the defense for some reason. "I have simply come to teach at the school." It wasn't quite true—at least, not entirely. He'd come for something far more important than simply teaching.

A servant entered the dining room to refill glasses and set more food upon the table.

"Do you not know who my parents are?" Hannie asked Gideon.

Brom shot a displeased look at his daughter.

"Of course I know who they are," Gideon said. "Who doesn't know them now that Mr. Irving's story has made them famous?"

"Famous?" Katrina fanned herself with her napkin. "Are we truly famous?"

"The story has met with wild popularity," Gideon assured her. "There are not many people in America who have not read or at least heard of it."

"Truly?" Katrina lifted her eyebrows. "And from such a silly little tale."

The short story had made a massive impact on the literature world—one that Gideon longed to make himself. For years, he'd been traveling the country, taking odd jobs as clerk, teacher, and the like, looking for his own stories to tell. He'd searched high and low, interviewed countless people, and had spent hours writing. He had found some minor success, though nothing compared to Washington Irving. When he'd read "The Legend of Sleepy Hollow," he knew he could never reproduce such a tale, but he had decided to come to North Tarrytown to gain inspiration and to see what Irving had seen. Maybe, if he was lucky, he could find some ideas. He'd inquired after the teaching position and had been shocked and surprised when Brom Bones himself had responded, as a member of the school board.

Now here he sat, in the very house where the frolic had taken place thirty-one years ago, that fateful night Brom Bones had frightened Ichabod Crane just hours before the Headless Horseman had driven the schoolmaster out of Sleepy Hollow for good.

"Well," Brom said as he lifted his crystal glass, "whatever brought you to North Tarrytown, we're happy you're here. Welcome, Gideon. May you find everything your heart desires right here in our little hollow."

Gideon readily lifted his goblet.

And noticed that Hannie did not lift hers.

Chapter Two

The evening had cooled, as it usually did in the gloaming hours of autumn. Hannie sat on the expansive porch, a thick shawl wrapped around her shoulders, as she listened to her father's deep, expressive voice. He didn't simply sit on his chair, but leaned forward, almost hovering, a smoking pipe in one hand while the other gestured wildly with his storytelling.

Mama sat on a rocking chair, her knitting needles moving almost of their own accord as a gentle smile tilted up her pretty mouth. Her eyes shone as she looked up from time to time, admiring her husband.

Gideon Webb also sat on the edge of his chair, his elbows on his knees, his hands clasped loosely together, listening intently to Papa's tales. Papa was most animated when he had a new audience. Most of his stories had been handed down to him from his forefathers, though others he'd experienced on his own—such as the one he had told Mr. Irving.

It was the story of the bird-like schoolmaster, Ichabod Crane, who had been in the hollow some thirty years past that Papa told tonight.

"For three months," Papa said, "Mr. Crane pecked about the Van Tassel farm, hoping to gain the attention of my Katrina. His eyes were not only on her, but on the bounty of this farm and the weight of the table, laden with the choicest foods in the country.

The pedagogue was easily frightened and had a mind for the supernatural. He was often seen with his copy of Cotton Mather's *History of Witchcraft* in hand and spent many an hour listening to the stories of the county."

The wind picked up, whistling low and long around the corners of the house. An owl hooted in the nearby woods, calling into the growing darkness. Clouds shifted over the waning moon, creating a filtered light on the landscape below.

Gideon sat up a little straighter, his gaze intent on Papa.

There was something otherworldly about the hollow, especially in the fading days of autumn, and men like her father made it more so. Hannie had grown up with the stories and the folklore, giving it little mind. But it never took long for a newcomer to believe the stories were true—or, at the very least, intriguing.

"The night of the frolic," Papa continued, "I knew Mr. Crane's intent was to propose. I saw it in the way he eyed my sweet Katrina and kept her in his sights all evening. It was easy enough for me to contrive a story to scare him away."

"You made up the story of the Headless Horseman?" Gideon asked.

Papa shook his head. "The Headless Horseman was a combination of several legends I have heard since I was a boy, but that night, he became bigger and more sinister than ever before. The more I talked, the more anxious Ichabod became, so the more I elaborated. Later, when I was helping clean up after the frolic, I saw him corner Katrina. He made his plea and was soundly turned away. I couldn't help but jump on my horse and play a little trick on him— one he wouldn't soon forget. I didn't think it would scare him so much that he'd leave Sleepy Hollow for good, but I didn't mourn his departure either."

Papa laughed, Mama blushed, and Gideon looked between them with amazement, making Hannie wonder.

If he had come to Sleepy Hollow to woo her and claim the farm, then why wasn't his undivided attention directed toward her? All throughout supper and then as they sat on the porch, he had given her very little notice. Other than a customary comment here or there, he had shown no interest in her company.

Hannie had expected him to treat her like all the other young men who had come clamoring for her hand in marriage. Their attentiveness had been cloyingly sweet and had never felt sincere. She detested it, but had come to expect it.

Gideon Webb was different. Though she had noticed his reaction upon meeting her, the way he had taken her in, appreciation gleaming from his eyes, he had not paid her the slightest compliment or even tried to sit beside her on the porch.

From her position now, she had a good view of him—and what she saw pleased her, much to her chagrin. She had not wanted to find Gideon handsome, but it was a fact that was impossible to ignore. His attractiveness wasn't just physical, though his kind eyes were a unique shade of gray and his brow was distinguished. His magnetism came from the way he treated them. Kind, sincere, not fawning over either her wealthy parents or worse yet, their eligible, someday-wealthy daughter.

He fascinated Hannie—and for the first time in her life, she was the one hoping to get a little closer, hoping for a smile, a nod—anything to acknowledge that he saw her.

"The hour is growing late," Mama said as she tucked her knitting into a ball and shoved it inside her knitting bag. "I must turn in."

As she began to stand, so too did Papa and Gideon.

"You stay and enjoy the evening," Mama said to Gideon as she put her hand on his shoulder and pushed him back in his chair.

Papa tapped his pipe on the palm of his hand. "We will save the other stories for another night."

Hannie began to rise as well, but Mama touched her arm. "You stay and keep Gideon company. Tell him about the frolic we are planning in his honor and familiarize him with the names of the families he will be serving as the schoolmaster."

"It's late," Hannie protested, unused to her parents encouraging her to be alone with a young man. What would Gideon think? If he hadn't come to win her hand, would he presume her parents were throwing her on him? She, an old maid? It was embarrassing, to say the least.

"Late for us older folks," Papa said, "but for those who have not been kissed with the passage of time, the night is still young."

Hannie wanted to protest further, but her parents would only push harder. She took her seat again, thankful the darkness would hide the color of her burning cheeks.

"Good night," Gideon said to them. "Thank you for welcoming me into your home."

Papa and Mama hurried off the porch, as if being chased by the Headless Horseman himself.

It truly wasn't late. Would Gideon see behind their facade?

Neither Gideon nor Hannie spoke for several moments as the night sounds grew more pronounced. Hannie hugged her shawl about her shoulders, wishing for the warmth of the hearth.

"It's been a pleasure meeting you and your parents," Gideon finally said, breaking the silence. "I still cannot believe we have a family connection, though a loose one."

"You truly didn't know?" Hannie asked.

"I had no idea."

"Was it the story that brought you to this place?" For reasons she couldn't identify, she knew he had not come simply to teach.

He was quiet for a moment, but then he leaned forward. Her eyes had adjusted to the darkness, and she could see him plainly.

"I am a writer," he said. "Much like Mr. Irving, or so I like to fancy myself. His work has intrigued me and drawn me to this place. I know I cannot reproduce his story, but I long to be inspired like he was—to see the world that he saw in this hollow. Meeting your father, the one who told the story to Mr. Irving, is like meeting a legend. It's an honor. I'm already starting to feel the stirrings of this place within my soul."

"I've heard that it has a way of doing that to outsiders."

"Do you see why I've come, Miss Van Brunt?"

She studied him for a moment, not feeling self-conscious in the least. "I do."

He seemed to relax.

"And you did not hear from your father?" she asked.

Gideon sat up straighter. "*Should* I have heard from my father? I sense this is an important issue, though I cannot imagine why."

Her cheeks warmed again. She could not tell him the truth—could she? Eventually he would know, so why not lay it out for him now? Then the two of them could deal with it together. After all, they'd have to address the situation at some point.

"When my mother learned of your identity," Hannie began, "she and my father contacted your father. It appears that several letters have passed between them since."

"Is there something important I should know about these letters?" His voice was melodic, gentle and soothing to Hannie's ears. He did not have the sound of the hollow.

"I see no reason to keep it from you, since you will soon find out." Hannie cleared her throat and placed her hands in her lap, trying not to lose her courage. "It seems that your father and mine hope for an…arrangement between us."

Gideon did not say anything for several long heartbeats, and then he said, in a hushed tone, "Matrimony?"

She was thankful again for the darkness, which shielded her feelings from being known to him. Mama always said she wore her emotions on her face, plain to be seen. "I believe that is their wish."

He stood and walked to the edge of the porch.

Hannie held her breath, uncertain how he would react. They were strangers, after all, and a marriage seemed far-fetched. Yet marriages had been arranged for centuries this way.

"I have no home, Miss Van Brunt. I'm an itinerant teacher, with no real prospects at the age of thirty. One day I hope to make a living with my writing, but as of now, I am one step above a pauper."

Hannie also stood, her heart pounding. "I did not intend for you to think I support this idea. On the contrary, I think it a silly notion."

He turned back to look at her. "I did not mean to offend you."

"You haven't. I just wanted you to know what they have discussed. I learned of it only moments before your arrival. My parents will no doubt be playing matchmaker while you are here, and I wanted to warn you."

He leaned against the post, his gaze directed at her. "Warn me? Would marrying you be so very bad?"

There was a teasing quality to his voice, and despite the awkwardness of the situation, she found herself warming to him. She decided to tease him right back. "No, indeed. I would imagine that being my husband would be a grand adventure."

He chuckled, and then his voice became serious. "I wouldn't doubt that for a moment."

A noise sounded on the road, and they both turned to look in that direction.

Two men were approaching on horseback, one holding a lantern aloft.

"I wonder who that could be," Hannie said almost to herself.

Papa and Mama must have heard or seen the men's approach, because they were soon on the porch again, awaiting the arrival of their visitors.

The sheriff sat on the lead horse, his face somber, shadowed by the lantern he carried. The second man was just behind him, hidden from view. As the horses came to a stop in the yard, and the second man pulled abreast of the sheriff, Hannie frowned. She'd never seen him before. He was about her parents' age, if not a little older, with sharp features. He was dreadfully skinny, with long legs and arms. Under his hat were a large nose and a small chin with graying whiskers, but his eyes were obscured by the evening the shadows.

in Sleepy Hollow, New York

"Abraham Van Brunt," the sheriff called. "This is Obadiah Crane—brother of the old schoolmaster Ichabod Crane. You remember him, don't you?"

Papa took a step off the porch, his back to Hannie. "Of course I do."

"Good." The sheriff dismounted. "We need to talk."

Hannie didn't like the sound of the sheriff's voice, nor the eerie silence of Obadiah Crane.

Gideon stood, transfixed, as Mr. Crane and the sheriff approached the front porch. Moments before, he and Hannie had been having a conversation that had both surprised and captivated him. Had his father truly written to Brom, seeking a union between their children? If it had been anyone else, anywhere else, he would have been appalled by the idea. So then, why didn't the thought of being wed to Hannie Van Brunt make him want to run? He'd spent his entire adult life avoiding scheming mothers and eager young women. He could have easily tied himself down to any number of people or places along his journeys, but he hadn't. The lure of finding the perfect story had propelled him on each step of the way. He longed for adventures.

Perhaps, as Hannie had said, marrying her would be the grandest adventure of all. The greatest story of his life.

But those thoughts quickly faded from his mind as he waited to see why the sheriff had arrived with Ichabod Crane's brother.

"Brom," the sheriff said, "again, this is Obadiah Crane."

Brom extended his hand to Mr. Crane, but the other man kept to himself. Forcing Brom to drop his arm back to his side.

"Welcome, Mr. Crane," Brom said. "This is my wife, Mrs. Van Brunt."

"How do you do?" Katrina asked the stranger, offering a pleasant curtsy.

Mr. Crane didn't respond to her either.

"And this is our daughter, Hannie, and the new schoolmaster, just arrived today, Mr. Webb."

Mr. Crane glanced in their direction, but it was hard to see his eyes under the brim of his hat.

"Would you all like to come inside?" Brom asked, indicating the front door.

"Perhaps we should." The sheriff motioned for Mr. Crane to precede him.

Gideon wasn't sure if he should follow, but he didn't know what else to do. He held the door open for Hannie as she passed by, and for the first time, he noticed that she wore the scent of lavender. It hit his senses, making his head swim. She glanced at him, for the briefest moment, and an inexplicable feeling warmed his chest.

A lamp was glowing in the front parlor. Katrina turned the wick up, casting more light into the room. She stood close to her husband as the sheriff and Mr. Crane came to a halt.

Hannie and Gideon held back, stopping on the edge of the ornate rug. He didn't know if she was aware of how close she stood by him.

"Brom," the sheriff said, "I wouldn't have come out here so late in the evening if I didn't think this was a dire situation."

"Would you like to have a seat?" Brom asked, concern tilting his brow.

"What we've come to say won't take long." The sheriff glanced at Mr. Crane, who finally removed his hat, revealing a balding head and small, shrewd eyes.

His gaze drifted to Hannie. Something about the way he looked at her made Gideon feel suddenly protective. He moved a bit closer to her, wanting to shield her from that beady stare.

"Mr. Crane came into my office today," the sheriff said, "with some alarming accusations." He paused and glanced in Hannie and Gideon's direction. "Perhaps you'd like to have this conversation in private," he said to Brom.

"I'm not afraid of what you have to say." Brom lifted his chin. "Hannie and Mr. Webb are welcome to stay."

The sheriff continued. "Mr. Crane has come to Sleepy Hollow to demand justice for his brother."

Brom crossed his arms and tilted an eyebrow. "Justice? For what?"

"You killed my brother," Mr. Crane said, leaning forward, his words seething from his mouth. "And I demand justice."

"Killed your brother?" Brom pulled his head back in surprise. "I did no such thing."

"Thirty-one years ago," Mr. Crane said, "I lost touch with my brother. I'd always assumed he had gone west to teach, or some such thing. I've spent the past thirty-one years looking for him. So, when Mr. Irving's story was published, you can imagine my great surprise to see my brother's name in print. I realized that he did not go west. He would have written at some point to at least tell our mother of his whereabouts. One doesn't just disappear into thin air. It's clear that you killed him and disposed of his body so you could become the master of this property—through any means necessary."

"Don't be preposterous, man!" Brom said. "Your brother ran away as fast as his legs could carry him, because he was a coward."

It was the wrong thing to say. Mr. Crane's nostrils flared as he balled his skeletal hands into fists. "I would call you out if I knew I wouldn't end up in prison."

Brom took a step forward, obviously larger and more powerful than Mr. Crane. "I stand beside my words. He was humiliated by Katrina's rejection and by his cowardly behavior upon the road. He could never show his face in North Tarrytown again."

"So you admit you chased him down the road that night," Mr. Crane said, pointing his bony finger in Brom's face, "pretending to be the Headless Horseman."

"Everyone knows it was me." Brom stared hard at that long finger until Mr. Crane lowered his hand again. "But I didn't kill the man."

"That shall be for the sheriff to decide."

Brom looked to the sheriff. "You believe this man's lies?"

"I don't know what to believe, Brom. You were pretty reckless in your youth."

"Not so much as to kill a man!" Brom looked to Katrina. "After I threw that pumpkin at Ichabod, I came back to Katrina and asked her to marry me. I wasn't gone long enough to kill Ichabod and dispose of his body."

"You were gone long enough to kill him," Mr. Crane corrected. "Who's to say when you returned to dispose of him?"

"This is absurd." Brom crossed his arms again. "I want you to leave my house, Mr. Crane."

"I will go," the man said, "but you will be hearing from me again. I'm staying at the local inn, and I will not leave until you are properly convicted and sentenced for the death of my brother."

Brom grabbed the man by the back of his collar and hauled him to the front door. "Get out of here and don't come back!"

"Now, Brom," the sheriff said, following behind. "Don't do something that will get you arrested. You're already in enough trouble as it is."

"Trouble?" Brom turned to the sheriff, who was now in the entrance hall. "Are you going to go through with this ridiculous investigation?"

The sheriff put his hat back on his head and lifted his hands again. "A man went missing thirty-one years ago, and the last person to see him alive was you. It's my job to make sure nothing sinister happened."

Brom shook his head, color rising in his neck. "I did nothing more than scare Ichabod Crane, and you know it."

The sheriff pushed open the door and Gideon caught a glimpse of Mr. Crane mounting his horse.

"I'm sorry, Brom," the sheriff said. "I really am." He nodded at Katrina. "It's late, and I don't want to bother you more than I already have. I'll be back soon to talk to both of you."

He joined Mr. Crane and mounted his own horse.

They left the property, heading back to North Tarrytown.

No one said a word as Brom slowly closed the front door. He turned and looked at Hannie, concern tilting his brow. "It's not true, Daughter."

She went into his arms, placing her cheek against his chest. "I know it's not, Papa."

Gideon felt like an intruder, but he didn't know how to excuse himself without drawing more attention.

"I'm sorry for this trouble," Brom said, looking up at Gideon. "Not quite the welcome we had in mind for you."

Gideon nodded, unsure what to say.

As the little family began to talk in hushed tones, Gideon suddenly realized he might have found the story he'd been waiting for his whole life.

Chapter Three

Hannie couldn't sleep, so concerned was she with the arrival of Obadiah Crane. His accusation against her father was both startling and farcical. To think her father a murderer? Hannie had never met a kinder, gentler soul. Yes, he was loud and gregarious, but he was also compassionate, loving, and fiercely protective. He would never do anything to hurt anyone, let alone murder them.

Her parents had gone up to bed over an hour ago, but Hannie suspected they were not sleeping either. How could they? If she knew her parents, they were probably speaking in serious, hushed tones, discussing the accusation and what they would do about it.

But Hannie wasn't ready to let her parents shoulder this burden alone. If she told them what she planned to do, they would never allow it. They tried to coddle and shelter her every chance they got— but not this time. She was going to prove her father had not murdered Ichabod Crane, even if she had to do it all by herself.

Deep darkness had fallen over the land as Hannie stood near her father's large desk in his office. She had never entered this room without his permission. If he knew she was here now, he'd be upset. But this was the best place to start her investigation. Papa saved everything. He hated waste, which was one of the reasons why he was so prosperous. Everything had a purpose, and it was used until it couldn't be used anymore. This habit spilled over into his bookkeeping and files. He saved every scrap of paper, every receipt, every letter, every bill—anything that kept a record of some kind.

Papa had always been this way, so surely, if there was evidence of any kind to be found from thirty years ago, it would be in this room.

Quietly, she pulled open the top drawer of his desk and removed a file. He was meticulous with his records, but Hannie didn't know his system.

As she backed up, she bumped into his chair, causing a sharp pain to radiate up her leg. She couldn't help crying out, but she clapped her hand over her mouth, hoping her parents hadn't heard her. The house was large, and their bedchamber was nowhere near her, but the office was close to the kitchen and dining room. If they had come down for any reason, they could hear her.

They would never approve of her meddling in this situation.

She waited for a moment, quietly listening, and then began to page through the file by the light of the candles she'd lit.

"Hannie?" Gideon's voice filtered through the closed door. "Is that you?"

Her eyes opened wide. What was Gideon doing awake at this hour?

"I heard something—do you need help?"

Help? Perhaps she did need help. If there were two of them looking through Papa's records, wouldn't they go twice as fast?

She walked to the door and opened it slowly, conscious of the squeak it made on its hinges. "Why are you awake?" she whispered.

"I couldn't sleep. Your father told me to make myself at home, and I couldn't stop thinking about the boterkoek." He held up a slice of the cake Hannie had made for supper, his smile a little sheepish.

"I thought I heard you cry out, and after that unexpected visitor this evening, I didn't want to go back to bed without checking on you."

His thoughtfulness warmed her. "I'm well."

She opened the door wider and peeked into the hall. Seeing it was empty, she motioned for him to enter.

He hesitated. "I wouldn't want to impose."

"I need your help," she said quietly. "Please."

Gideon studied her for a moment, his gray eyes filled with a dozen questions.

She didn't have time to wait for him to analyze the situation, so she tugged on his sleeve and pulled him into the office, closing the door behind him.

"If your father found us here," he said, his eyes filled with concern, "he'd probably kick me out of the house—or worse, demand I save your reputation and make you my wife."

His words hurt more than he might have realized. "Would that be so horrible?"

She hadn't meant to ask him such a leading question. He stared at her, his cheeks flushing as he seemed to grapple with a response. "I didn't mean—"

"Never mind," she said as she went back to the desk. "I'm looking for evidence to prove my father did not kill Ichabod Crane. We don't have much time. When the sheriff comes back, he will want to question my parents. If I can prove Papa is innocent before he comes, then I can spare my parents shame or anguish."

Gideon stood in the center of Papa's office, his uneaten boterkoek in his hand, continuing to stare at her. "What do you think you'll find in here?"

"I don't know. A letter, a diary, something that might help." She was desperate and wouldn't sleep until she had proof.

"If you don't even know what you're looking for, this could take days or weeks—and you still might not find anything."

Tears threatened as she paged through ancient documents, some of them over a hundred years old.

Gideon was right. She leaned back and propped herself against Papa's desk, feeling weak and useless. "I have to prove his innocence."

Slowly, Gideon placed the boterkoek on the desk and came to stand in front of Hannie.

She looked up at him, wishing she could go into his arms like she had Papa's. She needed strength, reassurance, and someone else's confidence right now.

"I don't think you'll find what you're looking for in here," Gideon said gently. "I think the better course of action is to retrace your father's steps that evening and speak to the people who were there. Someone must know something that would help. You should get a good night's sleep and then start fresh in the morning, when your mind is clear."

Hannie nodded. "You're right. There were several people involved—people we could interview. We'll start—"

"We?" Gideon took a step back, shaking his head.

"I'm willing to admit I'm too close to the situation." Hannie took a step toward him. "My emotions are too frayed, and I'm not thinking clearly. You just said as much yourself." She didn't want to beg—but wanted to convince him to help her. "You're familiar with the story, but you're not as invested as the rest of us. You have the fresh eyes I need to see things from a different perspective." Her lips were quivering, so she pressed her mouth together and took a deep breath before saying, "Please."

Gideon ran his hand through his dark hair, his expression torn. "I'm new to Sleepy Hollow. I don't know if I should get caught up in the middle of something that doesn't concern me."

She tried not to feel disappointed, but she couldn't help it, and she knew her face revealed the depth of her emotion. Granted, she hardly knew the man, and could prove Papa's innocence on her own, but she *wanted* him to help her. Wanted him by her side, not only because his presence was reassuring, but because she longed to get to know him better. He was the first person to enter their home as a prospective suitor she wasn't tempted to toss out. If her parents truly desired for her to keep an open mind where Gideon Webb was concerned, shouldn't she spend time with him?

Hannie looked down at her hands, not wanting to force him to help, but praying that he would.

"You've had a difficult evening," Gideon said, his voice low and tender. "Try to get some sleep. I'll think about your request and give you an answer in the morning. Will that do?"

She finally looked up at him, hope springing anew inside her chest. The exhaustion hit her then, and all she could do was nod. She did need to sleep.

He gently cupped her elbow and led her to the door, and then he turned and snuffed out the lights—grabbing his cake before joining her in the hallway. Hannie waited for him, and they walked out together, down the hall, up the stairs, and then paused on the topmost landing in the darkness.

"Good night, Hannie," he said, his voice just above a whisper. He gave a slight bow. "I'll see you in the morning."

"Good night, Gideon." She loved the sound of his name on her lips.

As they parted ways, Hannie's hope started to waver. What if she couldn't prove Papa's innocence?

Gideon was awake before the rooster crowed the next morning. For a moment, as the fog of sleep cleared, he wondered if it had all been a dream. Sleepy Hollow, Brom Bones, Obadiah Crane... Hannie.

It didn't take long for his eyes to adjust to the faint light of dawn. Slowly, his bedchamber came into focus, and he saw the antique furniture, the green damask canopy above his head, and the matching papered walls.

His thoughts stayed on Hannie, and he smiled. A comelier lass he'd never met, but it was the way in which her thoughts expressed themselves upon her face that drew him to her. Last night, in the quiet of the office, he'd almost promised her the world if she would but smile again. He knew she was heartsore over the situation with Mr. Crane, and desperate to *do* something—but he hadn't been sure how to respond to her. He wanted to help, and yet, it would cause them to be in close proximity. And though every one of his senses begged him to stay by her side, his rational mind told him it wasn't a good idea. Hannie beguiled him, and if he let his guard slip, he was certain she'd capture his heart. And that was the last thing he needed. He had nothing to offer her. He had hoped that his writing would provide for him, but he still hadn't found his story—though he suspected that he might, very soon.

Perhaps helping Hannie would give Gideon the pieces of the puzzle he'd need to write about Brom Bones and Obadiah Crane. He wasn't sure how this story would play out, but he wanted to be a part of it.

More than that, he longed to ease Hannie's burden. He didn't know her well, but he suspected that she would not stop until she found the answer she was looking for. He could see it in the determination in her eyes last night. If he helped her, maybe he could offer a fresh perspective and they could find the answer together.

He just needed to protect his heart while working with her. He determined to do so.

Gideon jumped out of bed, ready to be of service to Hannie. The autumn term would not start for several more days, and he would have all the time he needed.

After getting dressed, he left his room and followed the scent of sausage, coffee, and baked apples.

Breakfast was on the table when Gideon entered the dining room.

Hannie pushed through the kitchen door, a platter in each hand, and stopped short at the sight of him.

Her cheeks were rosy, and her blond curls were peeking out from underneath her cap.

Gideon hurried to take one of the platters from her and set it on the table. "Good morning."

"Good morning." She put down an apple pie, still steaming hot from the oven. The scent of cinnamon wafted up to his nose. "Papa and Mama left for town just minutes ago. They said to tell you that you are welcome to any book in the library to pass the time. They will return as soon as possible."

"Had they planned to go to town?"

She shook her head, her eyes troubled. "Not that I'm aware of. They would not tell me why they were going, nor would they let me go with them."

He wanted to lighten her somber mood, so he looked at the table and shook his head. "There is enough food here for a small village."

"Mama was up hours ago. When she's upset, she buries herself in her cooking. No doubt we'll have a feast tonight." She motioned for him to sit as she took a seat across from him.

"I'm starving, so I will gladly eat my fill." He hesitated, not sure of his place. Usually the man of the family said grace. "Shall I pray?"

"Yes, please."

They both bowed their heads, and for a moment, Gideon wondered if this was what it would be like to share a table—and a life—with Hannie. He could get used to starting his day this way. Seeing her beautiful face across from him, listening to the cadence of her voice, waiting to see what she had to say.

Suddenly, he could think of no better way to start a day.

He said a prayer and they began to eat.

"What do you call this?" he asked, lifting his fork.

"*Pannenkoeken*. It's a simple batter of eggs, milk, and buckwheat flour."

It was fluffy and light, topped with sausage and cheese. A feast all by itself. "I've never eaten so well."

"These are all family recipes. Mama has a special book that only she and I are allowed to see." A faint smile lifted the edges of her lips. But it soon faded as she pushed aside her plate. "I cannot wait any longer. Will you help me prove my father is innocent?"

The hope in her blue eyes was all he needed to see. He nodded. "I will help you."

He saw the relief wash over her, and she grinned. "I knew you would."

"Did you?" He laughed. "I hardly knew myself."

"You're too kind not to help."

He looked down at his plate, not willing to acknowledge such a claim. "Where shall we begin?"

"I plan to go to the home of Hans Van Ripper tomorrow morning."

Gideon looked up. "Hans Van Ripper?"

"Do you know him?"

"From the story, yes. Ichabod Crane boarded with him."

"Sadly, Hans passed away several years ago, but his son still lives in their old home. Albert Van Ripper is not a pleasant man, but he might answer some questions."

"Didn't the story claim that Hans took possession of Ichabod's property after he left?"

"I believe so. I haven't read the story."

Gideon blinked in surprise. "You haven't?"

She shrugged. "I've heard my father tell the story so many times, I could recount it for you now. I saw no reason to read it."

"Do you know—has your father or mother read it?"

"I don't believe so."

"Then how do you know if it's true?"

Again, Hannie shrugged. "It doesn't really matter. I don't think any of Papa's stories are completely true. From what I've heard, all the important pieces are there."

"Didn't Ichabod use Hans's horse and his best Sunday saddle?"

"Yes."

"You are right, the Van Ripper home is the best place to start. Why not go today?"

"In all the commotion last night, I forgot to mention the frolic Mama and Papa are planning to hold for you tomorrow evening." Hannie wiped her mouth with a napkin. "To introduce you to the community. I promised Mama I would help her today, but tomorrow morning, I should be able to get away for a bit."

"Do you think they'll hold the frolic as planned?"

"Mama and Papa use any excuse to host friends and family, and I don't think much would make them cancel. Not even this."

"Yoo-hoo," came a voice from the front door.

Hannie closed her eyes briefly. Frustration and annoyance flitted across her features for just a moment before she hid her emotions away and stood to greet whoever had entered the house.

Gideon stood as well.

"Katrina? Hannie?" Three women entered the dining room, each one dressed similar to Katrina Van Brunt, in old-fashioned, Dutch-influenced gowns. They were matronly women, with gray threads in the hair under their kerchiefs and wrinkles around their eyes and mouths.

"Tante Eva," Hannie said as she rounded the table and kissed the first woman on the cheek. "Tante Gertrud and Tante Abigael." She kissed each one. "This is Mr. Gideon Webb, the new schoolmaster."

Gideon shook their hands. "It's a pleasure to meet you."

"These are my father's sisters," Hannie explained.

"We've just heard the news," Tante Eva said, clucking her tongue, "and hurried right over to see if it was true. Is Ichabod Crane's brother accusing your father of murder?"

Hannie sighed. "Yes. But Papa is innocent."

"Of course he is," Tante Gertrud said, removing her kerchief. "Is your mother here?"

"She and Papa just left. I'm surprised you didn't meet them on the road."

All three aunts looked at Gideon.

"You're *alone*?" Tante Abigael asked.

"Of course not. Salome is in the kitchen, and Margareta is upstairs cleaning the bedchambers." Hannie took several plates off the sideboard. "Sit and eat. You can tell us what you know of the accusation."

The aunts were easily mollified with the prospect of food, and they saddled up to the table and began to dish up their plates.

"I heard that Ichabod Crane went to Pennsylvania and became a schoolmaster there," Tante Gertrud said. "He took a wife and had a passel of children."

"I heard he was spirited away by the Headless Horseman," Tante Eva said. "And he was never seen again on earth."

"If you are very quiet," Tante Abigael added, "on a dark evening, you can hear his spirit singing and reciting by the old schoolhouse. You do remember what a fair voice he had, don't you, sisters?"

The other two ladies nodded as they ate.

"Surely you don't believe he was spirited away," Hannie chided. "The story about him going to Pennsylvania sounds more realistic."

"One never knows," Tante Eva said. "Obadiah Crane claims to have never heard from his brother again, so perhaps my theory is not such a far-fetched idea, after all."

"Talk like that will surely get my father in trouble." Hannie frowned. "If Ichabod Crane is truly gone from this world, and my father was the last to see him alive, what would most people surmise?"

Tante Eva waved aside Hannie's concern. "It's just a folktale, Hannie. Calm down and eat your pannenkoeken before it grows cold."

"I believe the other rumor that circulated thirty years ago," Tante Gertrud said, with more authority.

Gideon leaned forward, as did Hannie.

Tante Gertrud looked at each of them, clearly enjoying being the center of attention for a moment. "Some said it was Hans Van Ripper who murdered Ichabod when he discovered his best Sunday saddle had been trampled under the horses and left out to the elements."

"Why would Hans murder someone over a saddle?" Tante Eva asked.

"To take possession of Ichabod's belongings as recompense for the cost of the saddle, of course." Tante Gertrud took a bite of apple pie. Around her mouthful, she said, "Or, there were some other nefarious dealings between them that went bad, and it was a fit of rage that caused Hans to act."

No one said a word as Hannie glanced at Gideon. He couldn't be sure, but he had a feeling she was even more certain they needed to start their investigation at the Van Ripper home. And, judging by the look on her face, she wanted to go now.

⁓ Chapter Four ⌒

Mama and Papa had still not returned to the farm an hour after the aunts left, and Hannie was starting to worry. What could be keeping them so long? There was much to be done in preparation for the frolic, and Mama would want everything to be perfect. She always spent the day before a gathering cooking and cleaning like a frenzied whirlwind.

Hannie and Mama had been baking all week, setting aside extra pies, pastries, and breads in the pie cabinet to share with their friends and family tomorrow. Instead of baking more, Hannie decided to get a head start on the cleaning. Gideon had offered to help, but he was their guest, and she had told him it wasn't necessary. He wasn't easily deterred though. He insisted on helping her and Margareta, the chambermaid, move heavy furniture and haul the largest of the rugs outside to the clothesline where they would be beaten and aired.

Working together gave them the opportunity to talk. Gideon told Hannie about growing up in Massachusetts, the son of a vicar. "Mother died when I was young, and it was just Father and I in the little vicarage until I left home." Gideon used a large beater and thwacked at a rug with ease. Plumes of dust wafted up into the warm, October air.

Hannie stood on the other side of the folded rug, beating with rhythmic timing. She couldn't see Gideon, but she loved listening to his voice.

"Did you always know you wanted to be an author?" she asked.

"From the moment I read Daniel Defoe's *Robinson Crusoe* when I was a lad of ten. I was so swept up in the story, I couldn't believe it was a work of fiction and that it had been written over seventy years before I was born. I wanted to write stories that not only moved someone's emotions but withstood the test of time."

She understood his passion, though she had never felt so passionate for anything in her life, outside the farm. "I wish I was as courageous as you, to travel across the country in search of the story you were born to tell. I've always known where I belong. I was born on this farm, I was raised on this farm, and someday, I shall die on this farm." Her words sounded morbid, but they were not. It gave her comfort knowing she had already found her calling in life. "Though I'd love to see the world, I've always felt content knowing I have deep roots right here in the most beautiful place I can imagine."

Gideon stopped thwacking the rug. "And I admire that you know exactly where you fit. I've always felt adrift. I know I don't belong in the vicarage—but I don't know where I do belong. Perhaps looking for a story to tell has been an excuse to travel the world trying to find my place."

Hannie's movements slowed until she too stopped beating the rug. She asked gently, "Do you think you'll ever find your place?"

He looked over the top of the rug, his gray eyes assessing, studying, questioning. "I truly hope I do."

The conversation had become too serious. She smiled. "I believe this rug is finished."

"I'll haul it in."

"Shall I help you?"

"It's light enough."

"I'll start on the next one."

After Gideon rolled up the rug and hefted it to his shoulder, Hannie couldn't stop her gaze from following his every move.

She had quickly realized that he possessed both brains and brawn, a combination that she had found lacking in most other men who had pursued her.

The realization that she was admiring him made her cheeks warm, and she turned back to the other rug as he disappeared into the house. Margareta and Salome were inside dusting and washing windows and the farmhands were out harvesting Papa's potatoes, which left Hannie by herself.

A movement near the tree line made her pause mid-thwack. Her heart began to race as she recognized the man approaching her. He was tall and thin, with a hawk-like nose under his low-brimmed hat.

Obadiah Crane.

Hannie stiffened as he moved toward her. She wished her parents were home—or that Gideon was still outside. Had Obadiah been watching, waiting for Gideon to move out of sight?

She braced her feet and gripped the rug beater until her knuckles turned white. At least she had a weapon, if she needed one.

"Why have you come, Mr. Crane?"

He stopped close to her, his small eyes roaming over her figure, as if he had the right. In the light of day she saw the deep wrinkles lining his face, indicating his advanced age, and noticed he had rheumy eyes.

Finally, he took his gaze off of her and let it wander over the hills, fields, and buildings on the farm. "My brother wrote to me when he first came to North Tarrytown, describing this farm. He was quite taken with it, if I remember correctly."

"Many people are. I am not surprised that your brother would be smitten."

Obadiah shifted his gaze to Hannie again. "It wasn't the only thing he was smitten with." He moved closer to her.

Hannie's back was against the rug, and she had nowhere else to go. He smelled of dust and sweat and his clothes were wrinkled.

"I seem to remember my brother's mention of Katrina Van Tassel." Obadiah narrowed his eyes. "He mentioned that she was one of the biggest flirts in the county, but he could overlook it because he fancied himself in love with her—and she with him. He had planned to ask her to marry him."

"He did ask her." Hannie breathed hard through her nose. "But she turned him down and married my father instead."

"So I've gathered." Obadiah put one of his hands atop the rug, leaning closer to Hannie. "Your father inherited this farm from old Van Tassel, did he not? And who is next to inherit? You, I presume? Or your husband, rather."

She lifted her chin. "That is none of your concern."

"Perhaps it could be." His point was made clear as he offered a chilling smile.

Hannie moved away, never turning her back to him. "You are not welcome here, Mr. Crane. My father made that clear last night."

"He's not here to haul me away, now is he?" Obadiah moved toward Hannie again.

"I believe the young lady has told you to leave." Gideon was suddenly there, stopping beside Hannie, his presence the most wonderful thing in the world. He wasn't as tall as Mr. Crane, but he was muscular and had youth on his side.

"The new schoolmaster, are you?" Mr. Crane asked, standing a little straighter. "I suppose there have been dozens of you since my brother's murder."

"He was not murdered," Hannie said, taking a step forward, feeling braver with Gideon nearby.

"If it wasn't for your father," Obadiah said to Hannie, "my brother would be master of this farm and he would be alive and well. I plan to make your father suffer for what he took from Ichabod."

"It's time for you to leave," Gideon said, moving toward Obadiah. "If you don't go of your own accord, I will remove you by force."

"I'm leaving." Obadiah put up his hands. "But I'll be back. This has only just begun."

He turned and strolled away, as if he were enjoying an afternoon in the park.

"I'll see that he leaves the property," Gideon said to Hannie. "Did he hurt you?"

She shook her head, her hands and legs beginning to tremble now that Obadiah was gone. "No. I'm fine."

He placed his hand on her arm. "You're pale and trembling."

"I don't like that man. I don't trust him."

Slowly, gently, Gideon drew Hannie into his arms, wrapping her in a hug.

He was warm and strong, and he smelled of spices she didn't recognize. His embrace was nothing like her father's, yet she still felt protected and cherished.

"I'll finish up here once I make sure he's gone." Gideon pulled back. "Why don't you go inside and make yourself something warm to drink?"

She looked up into his kind gray eyes and smiled. "How about I finish the rugs and then I make both of us something warm to drink?"

He returned her smile and nodded. "I think that sounds like a wonderful plan."

Gideon left her to follow Obadiah down the lane.

If Gideon hadn't arrived on the farm when he did and Papa and Mama had been in town, she would have been all alone with that awful Obadiah Crane. A nervous shiver ran up her spine as she silently thanked God for bringing Gideon into their life at just the right time.

Gideon discreetly followed Obadiah. The man was on horseback, though he seemed to be in no hurry. On foot, Gideon was able to keep him within sight until he left the Van Brunts' drive.

Minutes after Gideon turned back to the farm, a carriage came up behind him with Brom and Katrina aboard. Brom pulled the geldings to a stop, causing them to prance and sidestep as they tossed their heads.

"We just passed Obadiah on the road," Brom said. "Was he here making trouble?"

"He tried. I followed him to ensure he left the property."

"What kind of trouble?" Katrina asked, looking toward the house as she twisted a handkerchief between her fingers.

"I'm not sure, but he was talking to Hannie when I stepped out of the house. She's fine, though a little shaken."

"Hop into the carriage, son," Brom said.

Katrina scooted over on the seat, and Gideon pulled himself up to sit beside her.

Brom tapped the reins on the backs of the horses, and they took off for the house.

The mansion sat on a rise, overlooking the surrounding property. The farm sloped downhill toward the Hudson, though the river was on the opposite side of the public road and could not be seen from the house.

It was an old home, but it was grand and impressive and had been lovingly cared for over the years. It stirred something within Gideon he'd never felt before.

The desire to belong.

Perhaps it was because of his conversation with Hannie while they beat the rugs, or because he felt a bond with this family though they'd only just met. Whether it was because of his mother's connection, the Van Brunts' generous hospitality, or because he knew all about them from reading "The Legend of Sleepy Hollow," he wasn't sure.

Whatever it was, it also made him feel protective of this family. He was more certain than ever that he wanted to help them.

"Did you have a productive trip into town?" he asked.

Brom and Katrina looked at one another.

"We went into North Tarrytown to make inquiries about Obadiah Crane," Brom explained. "Who is he? Where does he come from? Is he being honest about his brother's disappearance?"

"Anything could have happened to Ichabod," Katrina added. "Perhaps he did go west and died out there. Now, with the popularity of the story, Obadiah might be here to cause trouble for us—or to get something out of us."

Gideon thought about what he'd just overheard before he interrupted Obadiah. The old man had asked Hannie if her husband would inherit the farm, and when she told him it wasn't any of his concern, he'd suggested that it could be. Had Obadiah come to try and woo Hannie to take possession of the farm? He had mentioned that it should have belonged to Ichabod. Did he still think so? If that was the case, then why accuse her father of murder? Was he hoping she'd turn to him for support if her father was convicted? It seemed preposterous, but anything was possible.

"We don't want to trouble Hannie," Brom said to Gideon. "She needs to be spared as much as possible."

Gideon was certain that Hannie was a lot stronger than they gave her credit for.

"We won't discuss this around her," Brom added. "And we'd appreciate the same from you."

"We've determined to put it behind us and enjoy the frolic tomorrow," Katrina said. "There's much to occupy our time as we wait for Brom's inquiries to return."

"We spoke to the sheriff, and he said he has sent out some inquiries of his own," Brom continued. "We spent an hour with him, giving our testimony about what happened the evening Ichabod went missing. We wanted to spare Hannie from having the sheriff return to our house."

"What did the sheriff say?" Gideon needed as much information as he could to help Hannie. He was certain she would not let this matter drop as easily as her parents.

"He is obligated to continue the investigation because of Obadiah's accusations. Unless we can find proof of what happened to Ichabod after he left here, I am still the main suspect."

Katrina's gaze never left her husband as he pulled the carriage up to the house to drop her off.

"Try not to let Hannie see your worry," Brom said to Katrina as he helped her alight from the carriage.

She smiled and laid her hand on the side of his face, and then she walked into the house.

"I'll help you with the horses," Gideon offered.

"Good man." Brom pulled the carriage to the barn where they unhitched the horses and led them into their stalls.

Gideon took a curry comb and began to brush down the first horse while Brom did the same with the other.

"Have you had word from your father?" Brom asked.

"No, I have not." Gideon cleared his throat, needing Brom to know his thoughts concerning the matter. "But Hannie told me what he might be writing to me about."

Brom paused and looked up at Gideon. "And what is that?"

Unease trickled through Gideon as he focused on his task. He'd never had to have a conversation like this one before. "A possible marriage between myself and Hannie."

"And?"

"It is a bit of a surprise," Gideon admitted. "But it is an honor that you would desire such a thing from me."

Brom left his horse and walked over to Gideon. "Hannie is the most important thing to me. She's dearer to me than my very life. I would not offer her to anyone if I did not think he was worthy."

"I beg your pardon, sir, but you do not know me well enough to know if I am worthy."

"It only takes me five minutes to weigh the character of a man—and my impressions of him rarely change, no matter how long I know him. Through your father's letters, and then after meeting you in person, I knew. Hannie has no interest in marrying a man from the hollow. Though she's content to stay here on the farm, I've always known she wanted more—even if she won't admit it to herself. She needs someone who can offer her the world. I believe you are that man."

A nervous sweat broke out on Gideon's brow. "I wish I could be so confident in your assessment, sir. But I have nothing to offer Hannie—not even a house of my own—nor any prospect of one."

"All Hannie needs is a man who loves the Lord and has the desire to protect her and provide for her all the days of his life. The rest will fall into place."

"But I have no prospects to provide for her." He had been a failure in his life's chosen profession. It was embarrassing to admit it now.

"Come with me." Brom put his arm around Gideon's shoulders and walked him to the barn door. "Do you see all of this farm?"

"Yes."

"When I proposed to Katrina, I had nothing—only my love for her and my determination to make her proud of me. This farm was a gift from her father, one he entrusted to me, just like he entrusted Katrina to me. I was not worthy of any of it, and because of that, I fought to make myself worthy. I still fight for it, every day. And, by the grace of God, I have been successful."

"You are a blessed man."

"Indeed." Brom removed his arm from Gideon's shoulders. "One day, Hannie and her husband will also inherit this land, and I pray they will be good stewards of it as well. You see, this land belongs to God, and He loans it to us as He sees fit. It's not mine—it wasn't Baltus Van Tassel's before me. It is God's. And when you look at it that way, as if you are just a steward who is managing it for the next generation, you treat it differently."

Gideon nodded, liking Brom's perspective.

"If you choose to marry Hannie—more importantly, if she chooses you," Brom said, "then this land will one day be yours. That's all the prospect you need."

But was it the future he wanted? How did his writing fit in? Could he be both an author and a farmer?

"You don't need to answer me now," Brom said, slapping Gideon on the back. "Prayerfully consider what you should do. I will ask Hannie to do the same."

Gideon found himself nodding, though his head was spinning with all the things Brom had just said.

He had a lot to think about.

Chapter Five

The morning of the frolic dawned glorious and bright. Hannie helped clean up the breakfast dishes, feeling unsettled by her mother's silence where Obadiah Crane was concerned. Neither her mother nor her father would talk to her about their mysterious trip into North Tarrytown, no matter how much she questioned them. They also wouldn't discuss the investigation or whether or not the sheriff planned to return to the farm.

Instead, during supper last night, the mood had been festive and light while her parents had asked Gideon a dozen questions about his life before coming to Sleepy Hollow. There had been absolutely no talk of the pressing matter at hand. Eventually, Hannie had let her parents continue with the ruse, knowing she would be doing her own investigation soon.

"I plan to bake this morning," Mama said to Hannie. "We still need to make a *spekkoek*, which will take some time."

Hannie nodded, knowing how much her aunts loved the traditional spice cake that Mama made for her frolics. Several layers were fried instead of baked, and it was time-consuming.

"I won't need your help for a bit," Mama said as she took out her tins of cinnamon, cardamom, clove, and nutmeg. "Why don't you take Gideon for a ride? He'll be starting classes on Monday and won't have as much time to court."

"Mama." Hannie shushed her mother. "What if he hears?"

"Your papa spoke to him yesterday about the possibility of marriage."

"Oh?" Hannie tried not to sound too eager.

"He didn't agree to an arrangement, but he didn't say no either." Mama's cheeks were pink from pleasure. "I think all that man needs is a little nudge in the matrimonial direction."

Hannie nibbled her bottom lip, not sure if she wanted to give Gideon the nudge or not.

"Spend some time with him," Mama urged. "See if you're a good fit."

"Perhaps you're right." Hannie lifted her chin thoughtfully. It would provide a good cover for her and Gideon to ride into North Tarrytown to question Albert Van Ripper.

"I'm always right," Mama said with a smile. "I believe Gideon is helping your father carry potatoes down to the cellar. Your father wouldn't mind if you took Gideon away for a few hours. Just be back in time to help move the furniture in the parlor and prepare yourself for the frolic tonight."

Hannie placed a kiss on her mother's cheek. "I will."

The temperature had risen, but it was still pleasant as Hannie stepped out of the kitchen door and found Papa pulling the loaded wagon up from the barn. It was piled high with potatoes the hired hands had harvested yesterday. They would be stored in the wooden bins in the cool cellar over the long winter months to feed the family. The others would be sold in New York City.

Gideon stood near the open cellar door. He wore a dark frock coat over a pair of lighter trousers. His style was modern and pleasing, drawing Hannie's eye whenever she was with him. Though they had just been together at breakfast thirty minutes ago, he smiled at her as if he hadn't seen her all day.

She returned the smile, loving how her insides felt all warm and excited to be near him.

"Mama suggested we take a ride," Hannie said to him, thankful her father was still a little ways off and wouldn't hear. "I thought we could use the time to ride into town and visit with Albert Van Ripper."

Gideon glanced at her father and then looked back at her. "Your parents asked me not to discuss the investigation with you."

Indignation rose up in her, and she opened her mouth to protest, but he held up his hand.

"I didn't agree."

A smile returned to Hannie's mouth. "Good."

"But I told your father I would help him with the potatoes."

"Mama didn't think he'd mind if I whisked you away." She glanced at the kitchen door and then leaned forward. "I think she's hoping we'll use the time to court."

"Is that so?" Gideon looked down at the ground, clearly uncomfortable with her straightforward comment.

"I'm only teasing," Hannie said, trying not to let her hopes get too high. Gideon had given no indication that he approved of the matchmaking, and she should have no reason to believe he would.

They met Papa on the path and told him they were going to take a ride. Hannie was careful not to tell him where they were going, knowing he would never approve. Instead, he grinned and didn't seem at all surprised that they would ask to saddle two of his horses.

Perhaps he and Mama had planned the whole thing.

Within thirty minutes, Hannie and Gideon were on their way into North Tarrytown. Hannie rode sidesaddle on a tame mare, one of her favorites, while Gideon rode a gelding. The ride didn't take long as they followed the main road into town. To their right, the Hudson River sparkled with life, teeming with fishing boats and barges.

"What can you tell me about Hans Van Ripper?" Gideon asked Hannie as they rode under the speckled sunlight glistening through the autumn leaves.

"What I remember from Papa's story is that Ichabod Crane was boarding with Hans around the time he went missing. He borrowed an old horse and Hans's best Sunday saddle to take to the frolic on our farm. When Ichabod went missing, Hans became the executor of Ichabod's property. There were some clothing and personal items as well as a few books and a piece of paper with some scribbled poems written to my mother."

"And when did Hans pass away?"

"I remember him slightly from when I was young, so perhaps in the past ten to fifteen years. His oldest son, Albert, inherited his father's property and lives there now with his family."

"Do you know Albert well?"

"No. After Ichabod left the hollow, Hans removed his children from school, believing that the schoolhouse was no place for his family. His sons carried on that belief and did not send their children to school either. They keep to themselves as much as possible."

"Do you think he'll be likely to answer your questions?"

Hannie thought about the disagreeable Albert Van Ripper and shuddered. "I don't know, but I'll try as hard as I can to get him to talk."

Gideon smiled as he looked toward the river.

"What?" Hannie asked. "What makes you smile so?"

"You." Gideon turned back to meet her gaze. His gray eyes looked almost blue today, perhaps a reflection of the bright sky, or an indication of his good mood. "I've never met another woman who is so single-minded or determined. Most women of my acquaintance would have heeded their father's wishes and not taken on this task."

A sheepish smile tilted Hannie's mouth. She didn't speak for a moment, reveling in the way Gidon admired her. Finally, she said, "I don't like to defy my parents, but I'm not as weak and delicate as they like to think. I'm a grown woman with a mind of my own. I know I can help them, if they'd only allow me to."

Gideon's horse moved closer to Hannie's, almost within touching distance. "I know you are, and that's why I agreed to help you. I couldn't imagine you sitting at home, letting the world to go on without you. You're a heroine, and you are writing your own story."

She liked the sound of that. It was a lot better than being labeled headstrong or stubborn.

Soon, the Van Ripper farm came into view. It was not a large piece of property, but it was well cared for and maintained. The house sat near the main road, not far from the edges of North Tarrytown. It was a white, colonial-era home, with thin clapboard siding. Chickens ran through the farmyard as Hannie and Gideon pulled their horses to a stop near the back porch.

Mrs. Van Ripper came out of the house, wiping her hands on her soiled apron.

"Can I help you?" she asked, squinting and putting her hand up to shield her eyes from the midmorning sun.

"We've come to speak to your husband," Hannie said. "Is he home?"

"Aye." She lowered her hand, looking a bit skeptical. "He's fixing the flue on my kitchen stove. Been having trouble with it. Come on in."

Gideon helped Hannie alight from her horse. His hands were warm on her waist as he lowered her to the ground. She stood for a moment, mere inches from him, her breath catching in her throat at the look in his eyes. It was warm and intense—and full of unmistakable attraction.

Perhaps Gideon wasn't ready to commit to marriage, but it wasn't because he found her undesirable. She could see that plainly.

"Thank you," she whispered.

A quiet smile filled his gaze as he stepped aside and attached the horses' reins to a hitching post.

Together, they mounted the steps to the farmhouse.

With Gideon so close, Hannie would have to work hard to focus on the task at hand.

The Van Ripper kitchen was warm—or maybe it was the heat from the exchange Gideon had just shared with Hannie that left him feeling this way. He stood close beside her as they stepped into the house. The kitchen was spacious and clean, much like the rest of the farm.

An older man stood by the cast-iron stove, reconnecting the flue to the wall. He stopped what he was doing when they entered.

"Albert," Mrs. Van Ripper said, "you've got company."

Mr. Van Ripper pulled a handkerchief from his back pocket and wiped his soot-covered fingers before offering to shake Gideon's hand.

"I'm Gideon Webb," he said, "and I believe you know Miss Van Brunt."

"Sure," Mr. Van Ripper said. "Brom Bones's daughter."

Hannie nodded.

"What can I do for you?" Van Ripper asked, his face set in a frown. "I heard that Ichabod Crane's brother is in town, making some accusations."

"Unfortunately," Hannie said, "he is. That's why we've come."

Mrs. Van Ripper stood just behind her husband, watching with wary eyes. The couple were easily in their midforties, with graying hair at their temples and faint wrinkles lining their weathered faces.

"What would I have to do with Ichabod Crane's brother?" Van Ripper crossed his arms, tossing his irritated stare between Hannie and Gideon.

"Ichabod Crane was boarding here when he went missing," Hannie said. "We were wondering if your father ever spoke about him or heard where he might have gone after he left Sleepy Hollow."

Mr. Van Ripper frowned. "He might have mentioned him in passing once or twice, but once Crane left the hollow and Pa pulled us out of school, he probably didn't think much about the man."

"There were a few things that Ichabod left behind," Gideon said. "Some clothing and books. Some people claim your father burned everything, but we're hoping the rumors aren't true."

Van Ripper's frown deepened. "If there was anything, I never heard about it."

The look of disappointment on Hannie's face was so keen, Gideon's heart felt heavy for her. He knew how much hope she had placed on this visit.

"If the man left anything," Mrs. Van Ripper spoke up from behind her husband, "it might be in the attic. Albert's father put everything up there. Couldn't throw anything away. I've been meaning to clean out that attic for years but haven't had the time."

A light shone in Hannie's eyes again. "Could we look?"

"I don't know how it would help your pa," Van Ripper said, "but I don't care. It's a mess up there. It could take you hours to search."

"We have the time." Hannie nodded at Gideon, as if to confirm her statement.

Gideon couldn't hide the joy he felt seeing Hannie's excitement. Even if this search came to nothing, he was happy he could see her with a bit of hope. She looked so pretty in her gown with her hair curled at the edges of her face. He could admire her all day.

"I'll show you up to the attic," Van Ripper said. "Though it's probably a waste of your time."

They followed him through the kitchen, up a set of stairs, and then waited as he opened a squeaking door to reveal another stairway up to the attic.

"I'll be out in the barn if you need me," Van Ripper said and then left them.

Hannie practically skipped up the stairs with Gideon close behind her. Natural light poured into the attic from windows on either end of the long room. The ceiling slanted down on each side, revealing nails poking through the boards.

The room was full of boxes, furniture, and trunks. A layer of dust covered everything.

"Where in the world should we begin?" Gideon asked.

"Look for a small trunk or traveling valise. I imagine Ichabod brought one along with him when he came." Hannie was already moving items aside as she lifted one thing after the other.

Gideon scanned the room and noticed a stack of luggage near one of the windows. He picked his way through the mess until he reached the valises. Slowly, he opened one after the other, looking through the various items in each one.

It was the third valise that made him pause. Inside were two shirts, two stocks for the neck, two pairs of stockings, a pair of corduroy knee breeches, a razor, a book of psalms, a pitch pipe, and three books, including one of dreams and fortune-telling, one titled *New England Almanac*, and Cotton Mather's book, *History of Witchcraft*. There was also a piece of paper, yellowed with age, that had several poetic verses, presumably written for Katrina.

"Hannie!" Gideon shouted, not realizing his voice would carry so well across the attic. "I think I've found it."

Hannie glanced up, her eyes wide. She climbed over several boxes, picking up her skirts in her haste to get to his side. She nearly tripped once but stayed on her feet and took the valise out of his hands before he could contain his chuckles.

"I knew it would be here!" She grinned as she looked through the items.

"What do you think you'll find?"

"I don't know, but something. Perhaps something that will tell us where Ichabod went—or, if Hans Van Ripper was guilty of murdering him, like Tante Gertrud suggested."

Gideon paged through the book of psalms while Hannie looked through the *New England Almanac*.

"Nothing looks out of the ordinary or suspicious," Gideon said.

"There has to be something here to help us." Hannie set down the almanac and picked up the *History of Witchcraft*. She opened the front page and then said, "Look! Here's something."

She held the book open for Gideon to see.

"To Ichabod, love Mother." Hannie read the inscription out loud. "1785, Greenwich, Connecticut."

"Greenwich?" Gideon asked. "Do you think that's where Ichabod came from?"

"I remember Papa saying that Ichabod came from Connecticut. Greenwich is less than twenty miles east of North Tarrytown."

"Perhaps he still has family in Greenwich."

"We have to go," Hannie said, flipping through the rest of the book.

"Home?" Gideon asked.

"No." She looked up at him. "Go to Greenwich. Tomorrow. We've no time to lose."

"Hannie." Gideon put his hand on her arm to still her. "We can't go to Greenwich."

"Why not?"

"What would your parents think? They'd never allow it."

"They wouldn't need to know. We can leave before they wake up tomorrow. I'll write them a note and tell them I'm with you and not to worry."

He frowned. "I cannot take you without their consent."

"I'll tell them in the note that we've gone on another ride. It won't be a lie."

"What if they learn the truth?"

"If you won't come with me, I'll go alone."

Frustration welled up inside him. He admired her determination, but he didn't like how stubborn she was acting. "Why don't we tell the sheriff and let him go? It's his job, after all."

"It could take him weeks before he goes to Greenwich, and we'll have to put up with Obadiah Crane until this matter is cleared. He frightens me." A shiver ran through her. "I want him gone as soon as possible. Greenwich is only twenty miles. We can be there in the early morning and be home by afternoon."

Just thinking about Obadiah Crane and the way he had cornered Hannie yesterday made anger course through Gideon. He wanted Obadiah gone too. They probably could get to Greenwich and back by the afternoon—and hopefully have more information for the sheriff.

"If I agree," Gideon said, "we cannot dillydally for even a moment. We must get you home as soon as possible."

Hannie nodded. "Of course."

"And what will we tell your parents?" He shuddered to even think about Brom Bones being angry with him.

"Leave that up to me. If we find the information we need to clear Papa's name, he won't care that we were gone for a few hours."

"It will be more than a few hours. It will take us at least two hours to get there, if we ride fast, and two hours to get back. There's no telling how long it might take us in Greenwich to find Ichabod's mother—or any other family member—*if* they still live there."

"I have a good feeling," Hannie said. "Just like I did about finding something here in the attic. I know we'll get the answers we need."

He gave her a look. "I hope you're right."

When she smiled at him, like she was doing now, there was very little chance he could say no to her.

As they moved through the attic to get back to the stairs, Hannie stopped. "What is this?" she asked as she picked up a thick book. "It looks like a diary."

She handed Cotton Mather's book to Gideon and then thumbed through the diary.

"Look!" She pointed to a page. "This is Hans Van Ripper's daily log book. And this date is the thirtieth of October, 1790, the day after Ichabod went missing."

"What does it say?" Gideon stepped closer to Hannie to look over her shoulder. She smelled like cinnamon and vanilla. A heady combination.

"It looks like he wrote in it almost every day, just little tidbits, mostly mundane. It says that he was in New York City on the twenty-ninth, conducting business. He did not return until the next day. When he got home, his family told him the schoolmaster had not returned since the night before, so he retraced the road to the Van Tassel farm, and that's where he found his saddle, alongside Ichabod's hat and a smashed pumpkin. They searched the nearby creek for the body, but finding none, assumed the teacher had left of his own accord."

"So," Gideon said, "Hans Van Ripper wasn't even in Sleepy Hollow the night Ichabod went missing."

"Which means he couldn't have killed him."

"That's what I was thinking." Hannie set the diary back on the shelf where she'd found it. "If we need this information, we know where it is."

Gideon didn't want to remind Hannie that if Hans Van Ripper was innocent that left only one other suspect. Her father—unless they wanted to believe the spirited tales of the Headless Horseman whisking Ichabod away.

"Tonight is the frolic," Hannie said as Gideon followed her down the steps. "And tomorrow, we ride to Greenwich. I *know* we'll find something important there."

Gideon might have shared her optimism if he wasn't so worried about what Abraham Van Brunt would think when he realized his daughter had left town with the new schoolmaster.

Chapter Six

In all her life, Hannie had never attended a livelier, more festive frolic than the one her parents hosted that evening. Perhaps it was the abundance of good food spread out on the table and sideboard in the dining room, or the new fiddle one of the musicians played, or even the sheer number of people who had come.

Or maybe it was because of Gideon.

Hannie was just as much a hostess as her mother that evening, greeting friends, neighbors, and family members as they arrived, replenishing food as it was eaten, and visiting with their guests as they danced and ate. But no matter where she went within the main floor of the house, she always knew where Gideon was standing.

He had been a popular addition to their frolic. Everyone was eager to meet the new schoolmaster. It didn't hurt that he was handsome and easy to talk to. Hannie noticed several eager mamas presenting their marriageable daughters to him. As usual, he appeared kind and attentive—though Hannie didn't like it one bit. Her feelings for him had grown unexpectedly in the past few days, surprising her with their depth. She'd never once felt an inkling of jealousy over any other man who had tried to court her—so why now?

The only thing that gave her hope was the fact that he also seemed to know exactly where she was throughout the evening. Their gazes caught often, and when they did, they shared a private smile, no matter how much space separated them—and no matter who they might be speaking to at the moment.

As the evening progressed and Papa gathered a circle of eager young ears to listen to his stories in the dining room, the dancing began in earnest in the parlor. All the furniture had been pushed against the walls or moved to other parts of the house to make space. The rug had been rolled up, and the musicians were tucked into a corner, out of the way.

It was a tight squeeze with the number of occupants, but it didn't dim anyone's enthusiasm. If anything, it added to the gaiety.

"Mr. Webb has been here for three days?" Martha Foshay asked, leaning toward Hannie. She was one of Hannie's best friends since childhood and had been married for four years now, with two little ones in tow.

"Aye," Hannie said, lifting little Mirabelle into her arms and giving the toddler a hug.

"He's handsome and well educated?"

"He's the new schoolmaster. I hope he's educated."

"More importantly," Martha said with a knowing smile, "he can't seem to take his eyes off you."

Hannie looked up to find Gideon across the room, a plate of food in hand, while an older woman spoke to him. He nodded at the woman but glanced up in Hannie's direction, awareness in his gaze.

It made a pleasant shiver ride up Hannie's spine.

"So?" Martha asked as she adjusted her baby to her other hip. "What's happening between the two of you? I've seen your mother and father both send approving looks in your direction as well. Is there something I should know?"

Hannie offered a sweet biscuit to the toddler and bussed her cheek. She had always shared everything with Martha, but this time—this time she wasn't sure what, if anything, she was ready to share. Her growing feelings for Gideon were so new and unexpected, she didn't want to spoil them with conjecture and speculation. She wanted to hold them tight, reveling in the way they made her feel. Both lighter than air and more grounded than she'd ever been in her life. The sensation was delectable and heady and so many other things Hannie had never expected.

"Will you not tell me?" Martha asked.

Hannie glanced at Gideon again, wishing he would ask her to dance. "Nay," she said to her friend. "I will tell you nothing, for there is nothing to tell." And there might never be anything to tell if Gideon had no interest in her.

Tom Van Ecker approached Hannie, his hair smoothed back, wearing his best breeches and tailcoat. His eyes were alight with hope. "May I have this dance, Miss Van Brunt?"

He was one of several young men who had asked her to dance. As the hostess, she was obligated—though she would rather not. Tom had been pursuing her since she was seventeen, and he had made no effort to court anyone else. She didn't want him to continue to hope, but neither could she be rude.

"Of course." Hannie set Mirabelle down and took the hand that Tom offered. The musicians began a lively reel and Tom grinned like a smitten fool.

"When will you agree to marry me and put me out of my misery?" he asked her as they followed the steps of the country dance.

"I will never agree, Tom." Hannie turned and found herself nearer to Gideon than she'd been all evening.

He smiled at her before his gaze shifted to Tom.

As she came back around, she faced her dancing partner again and noted the disappointment in his brown eyes.

"I've been patient for seven years, Hannie. It's driving me to distraction. I can think of nothing else but you. I want to start our lives together."

Again, they turned out, and again, she was near Gideon. Could he hear what Tom was saying to her? Embarrassment filled her chest and warmed her cheeks.

"You must not say such things," Hannie whispered vehemently to Tom the moment they were facing one another again. "I won't dance with you a second time if you insist on speaking of this."

He looked chastised but nodded.

A new arrival appeared in the parlor. The sheriff stood with a glass of punch in hand, watching the dancers. Had he come to question Papa further? Or was he simply there as a guest? The frolics were open to one and all, so it wasn't unusual to see a surprise visitor, though it made Hannie uncomfortable.

Unease twisted her stomach, making her lose what little appetite she'd had—not only for food, but for the frolic in general. Tomorrow, she and Gideon would leave before dawn to make their way to Greenwich. She had been confident and sure of herself while standing in the Van Rippers' attic—but now? Hours before they were to leave, with the sheriff there to make it all so real, she wasn't feeling as certain. It was unlikely that Ichabod Crane's mother was still alive or that there were people in Greenwich who would know what happened to the man. Mama and Papa would be angry that she left—alone—with Gideon, though she knew they would forgive her, especially if she found important information.

But so many things could go wrong.

Yet when she looked at Gideon again, she saw that he also studied the sheriff. He glanced in her direction and gave her a reassuring smile. Knowing that he would be with her tomorrow gave her the burst of confidence she needed. Surely, with both of them working together, they could solve this mystery.

They had to.

The reel ended and Tom bowed before another young man arrived at Hannie's elbow to ask for the next dance. Hannie obliged, hoping and praying that Gideon would soon ask her. She didn't want the evening to pass without dancing alongside him at least once.

Outside the house, the wind picked up intensity, shaking the windowpanes. Hannie noted the change, wondering if foul weather was on the way. It would not bode well for traveling in the morning.

Papa's voice could be heard between the dances as he regaled his audience with stories of the Headless Horseman. He sat in an ornately carved chair, near the large windows in the dining room, a pipe in hand. She could imagine his bright eyes as he spoke. The legend of the Headless Horseman was quite popular and one of his favorites to tell. His face always became animated as he told of the Hessian solider who had lost his head from an American cannonball during the Battle of White Plains on October 28, 1776. The soldier's body was buried in the Old Dutch Church cemetery in Sleepy Hollow and legend held that around the anniversary of his decapitation, he rose from his grave, wielding a pumpkin as a temporary replacement for his head.

"I once met the Galloping Hessian when I was a younger man," Papa said, his tone lowering with a drowsy note, as if he were mentioning a meeting with a neighbor. "I was on my way home from Sing Sing when he overtook me on the road. I offered to race him for a bowl of punch, and I would have won too, if he hadn't disappeared in a flash of fire as soon as we reached the wooden bridge near the Old Dutch Church."

Disbelief and excitement echoed off the lips of the young audience.

"If you should ever meet the Headless Hessian of the Hollow," he warned his listeners, "run or ride as fast as possible to the bridge. If you make it before him, he will disappear, and you will have won the race."

Hannie shook her head. Some things never changed.

The room had become warm and close with the press of people, but Gideon didn't mind. He still couldn't believe he was in the old Van Tassel mansion, attending a frolic, listening to Brom Bones share folktales about the Headless Horseman. It was almost as if he were a character in the story.

He'd met so many people, he couldn't possibly remember all of their names. Enthusiastic mothers had paraded their beautiful daughters before him all evening, and many of the young ladies had batted their eyes and let it be known they were a prize to be won.

But none of them had captured his attention—because it was fully devoted to the only woman who had made his pulse skitter in years.

Hannie Van Brunt looked stunning in her blue gown with its tightly cinched waist and lightly puffed sleeves. The color made her eyes luminous and bluer than the sky on a crisp autumn day. She laughed and teased as she worked her way through the guests, meeting their needs, stopping to visit here and there, lifting a child to offer a treat. Her face glowed, making her the most beautiful woman Gideon had ever beheld.

And he knew his heart was lost forever.

The realization made him sit up a little straighter, his pulse galloping like the Hessian in Brom's story.

How had he fallen in love so soon? Or so profoundly? He hadn't been looking for love—if anything, he'd been looking to avoid it. But here he was, completely besotted by the young heiress.

Surely he wasn't the only one. A half dozen young bucks had been pawing around Hannie all evening, and though she was aware of them, she didn't appear to notice the depth of their ardor. How had none of them won her heart before now? And why did he hope he might have a chance?

"Are you enjoying yourself?" Katrina was at Gideon's side, coming up to him without his notice.

"It's been a wonderful evening. I've never eaten such delicious food as I have since coming here. Are all the cooks in the hollow as good as you?"

Katrina's cheeks colored pink and she shook her head. "Oh, how you tease me."

"I'm not teasing," Gideon protested. "The food is like nothing I've ever eaten before. You are, quite possibly, the best cook and baker in America."

She laughed outright and playfully swatted at his arm. "That's a bold statement to make, Mr. Webb. Besides, most of the food you've sampled is Hannie's doing, not mine. I've taught her everything I know, and she's taught me a few things too."

"Hannie?" Gideon turned to admire her, noting another young man dancing with her.

"She's beautiful tonight, isn't she?" Katrina asked, tilting her head. "A rare treasure."

Gideon smiled to himself, though his longing to hold Hannie in his arms increased with each passing moment. He'd already imagined what it would feel like to kiss her under the harvest moon and tell her that he was falling in love with her. His pulse ticked higher at the very thought, and he had to look down, afraid his face would betray his feelings.

"Why haven't you invited her to dance?" Katrina asked. "I can tell she's waiting."

Was she? "I am not a good dancer. I would embarrass her."

"I doubt that." Katrina laughed. "Have you seen the men who have danced with her tonight? Even if you had two left feet, you'd be a vast improvement. Besides…" She lowered her voice in a conspiratorial tone. "I have a feeling that no matter how you dance, Hannie will only be aware of the fact that your arms are around her."

Gideon gaped at Katrina, surprised at how freely she, Brom, and Hannie spoke of such delicate matters.

Katrina laughed. "Don't look so astonished. I'm only saying what I know to be true." She patted his arm. "Don't let more time pass. The frolic won't last all night."

As Katrina moved away and the current song came to an end, Gideon forced himself to move across the space to intercept Hannie before another man stepped in line.

She turned, a breathless smile on her face, and almost fell into Gideon's arms in the crush of people.

"Oh," she said, a delightful smile lighting up her face.

People pushed from each side, pressing them closer together. Gideon's hands were on Hannie's arms, though he couldn't remember how they'd gotten there. Had he reached out to steady her?

It didn't matter. They were there now, and he didn't want to move them.

"Is this next dance spoken for?" he asked, his voice lowering for her ears alone. "Or am I too late?"

She blinked up at him, her thick lashes appearing darker tonight than usual. Slowly, Hannie shook her head. "You came just in time."

Gideon wanted to pull her into his arms right there, but it would be indecent and would make a scene. Instead, he swallowed and took a deep breath, hoping he wouldn't make a fool of himself.

The musicians began a quadrille, the first of the evening.

She looked up at him, studying him in the dim lighting. "Shall we begin?"

Gideon forced himself to move his feet, though they felt like large boulders. It took a few moments, but eventually they were turning with the other couples. She moved like silk and satin, smooth and gentle, as gracefully as a swan upon a lake. Her poise should have made him feel clumsy, but it didn't. It had the opposite effect, giving him the sensation of walking on clouds.

They didn't speak for several moments as they found their rhythm. Hannie's emotions were usually so easy to read, but at the moment, he couldn't identify the look in her eyes.

"What?" he finally asked her, when they came together again.

"You," she said, mimicking his response to her earlier that day.

"Me?"

"You're nothing like the others, are you?"

He didn't know how to answer her. Everyone liked to believe they were unique and nothing like their peers. But he wasn't foolish enough to actually believe he was different.

"I'm simply a man," he said to Hannie, "with a calling on my life and a lot of unanswered questions."

A slow smile grew on Hannie's lovely face. "I like you, Gideon Webb. Very much."

He couldn't stop himself from smiling, even if he had wanted to—and he didn't. "I like you too, Hannie Van Brunt. Very much."

It wasn't a confession of love, but it was almost as sweet and fulfilling. He *did* like Hannie, and he was pleased beyond reason that she liked him too.

Before he was ready, the song was over.

"I don't want this to end," he said to her.

They stopped as the others milled about them, finding their next dancing partner.

"What do you propose, Mr. Webb?" Hannie asked, her voice hushed as she kept their eye contact unbroken.

"Can we go onto the porch and talk? Would anyone mind?"

"Some of the young men might mind," she said with a chuckle. "But they'll be fine."

One of those young men was on his way through the crowd, his gaze intent on Hannie.

Without another thought, Gideon took her by the hand and led her to the front door.

The night had grown as black as ink. Clouds covered the vast sky, blocking out the moonbeams that had lit the landscape the two previous nights. It was colder, though not unpleasant, as they stepped out the front door.

"Do you need a shawl?" he asked, close beside her.

"I'm so warm, I don't think I'll need anything tonight."

There was no one else on the porch as they moved away from the door, still close to each another, and stood by one of the porch posts. Her arm brushed against his, but neither moved.

So many thoughts were crowding his mind, making it hard for him to know where to begin. He had only known her for a few days. Was it foolish to discuss the future? Was he even certain that he had it within him to make her happy? Could he take over the farm one day and make it prosper as Baltus and Brom had done before him? The last thing he wanted was to disappoint Hannie.

She didn't speak either, as she looked out across the property.

Crickets sang with the wind, serenading them with a song as old as time.

Finally, Hannie looked up at him. His eyes had adjusted, and he was able to see her clearly.

"This is so much better," she said, her voice just above a whisper. "I'd rather be here alone, with you."

His pulse skittered, and he leaned a little closer to her, wishing he had answers to quell the questions in his mind and heart. He didn't know much, but he knew he wanted to kiss her. Of that, he was quite certain.

But what kind of cad kissed a girl he wasn't ready to marry?

Instead, he lifted his hand—slowly, so she would have time to pull away—and gently touched her cheek. Her skin was softer than he imagined, like the petal of a delicate flower.

Her breath caught and her eyes looked larger than ever before.

He swallowed hard. "Hannie—"

"Yes?" She blinked several times.

Slowly, he removed his hand and took a step back. He couldn't continue to touch her and not kiss her—it would be impossible. And, until they were ready to commit to one another, he would never cross that boundary.

The disappointment on her face told him all he needed to know. She wanted him to kiss her—possibly propose as well.

"I'm sorry," he said, running his hand through his hair and turning away from her.

A piece of paper, folded into thirds, sat under a large rock on one of the side tables. It gleamed even in the darkness. Gideon picked it up and saw Hannie's name scrawled in a spidery script on the front.

He handed it to her.

"Is this from you?" she asked.

"No. I just found it here."

She went to a window where light spilled out and slowly unfolded the piece of parchment.

Her lips parted and she shook her head.

"What is it?" he asked, joining her.

"It's from Obadiah." She pushed the letter toward Gideon and then walked back to the post, wrapping her arms around herself.

Gideon lifted the paper and read the short note.

> Hannie,
>
> I have come to Sleepy Hollow to avenge my brother and to take what should have rightfully been his. I will do whatever it requires. I know we can be happy together, and as soon as your father is convicted, I will make you my bride. You have my word.
>
> Obadiah Crane

"He must have been here," Hannie said, motioning to the window. "He was probably watching us inside. For all I know, he's watching us now." She turned her back on the farmyard and moved to the door. "I cannot live like this, always wondering when he'll show up next."

Gideon met Hannie at the door, wanting to protect and reassure her. "We'll find more answers tomorrow," he promised. "I won't rest until he's gone."

She looked up at him and nodded, just once, before she stepped back into the house.

As the door closed behind her, Gideon crumpled the paper in his fist.

He'd made a fine mess of things.

Chapter Seven

It wouldn't be light out for another hour. Hannie tried to cover her yawn as she mounted her mare in preparation to leave. It had been late by the time their last guest had left the night before, and then she had helped to restore order to their house before she went to bed. Though she had been exhausted, she hadn't slept well, tossing and turning for hours thinking about how much she had wanted Gideon to kiss her.

And how much she wanted to be free of Obadiah.

No matter how tired she was this morning, she was more determined than ever to prove Obadiah Crane was a liar. She'd considered telling her parents about Obadiah's note, but she didn't want to worry them. Her father had enough trouble to deal with right now.

"The weather doesn't look like it will hold," Gideon said as they turned their horses out of the farmyard and headed toward the main road.

Hannie glanced up at the ominous sky and repositioned herself on the sidesaddle. "Then we'll need to move faster." She tapped the side of her mare, forcing the horse to pick up speed.

Gideon wasn't far behind.

Things had been awkward between them after their foray on the porch. She felt like a fool, thinking he might kiss her or declare his intentions. Instead, he had taken a step back and disappointment had rushed through her—disappointment and embarrassment. Had she been hoping in vain?

The letter from Obadiah hadn't made things any better. Thinking about it made her shiver. What was the man capable of? Would he truly not rest until he had what he wanted?

They rode for almost an hour without saying an unnecessary word to each other. The weather held and the clouds began to clear. Hannie had been to Greenwich before and knew which way would be fastest. Gideon followed, close to her side.

Slowly, the sky began to change. A hint of yellow on the eastern horizon grew, turning the dome overhead from black to gray to yellow, and finally blue.

Hannie struggled to stay awake. She swayed on her horse several times and nodded off once, pulling herself upright with a jerk. The cold penetrated her jacket, and the overhanging branches on the road caught in her hair and scratched at her cheeks.

But none of that was as bad as the embarrassment she still felt from Gideon's rejection last night. As the time passed, her mood turned more and more foul.

"Why don't we stop for a few minutes and stretch?" Gideon asked, breaking the silence between them as he reined his horse to a stop.

They were still on a well-traveled road, surrounded by trees on both sides. It was much like a tunnel, the leaves displaying brilliant colors and floating slowly down to the road.

"I don't want to stop," she said as she kept moving. "The longer it takes, the more upset my parents will be."

"You told me you would deal with them," he said as he tapped the sides of his horse and caught up to her. "Did you leave them a note?"

She had meant to leave them a note, but she and Gideon had been thirty minutes away from home by the time she realized she had forgotten.

"They'll understand when I explain it to them later," she said.

"And until then, they'll be sick with worry." His voice had taken on a frustrated tone. "They'll probably send out a search team to look for you."

"They'll do no such thing."

"Oh?" he asked. "Do you disappear with men all the time?"

Hannie scowled at him. "What do you think?"

"I don't know what to think, Hannie. I agreed to come under the agreement that you would leave a note for your parents. I knew they'd still be upset, but at least their fears would be alleviated. I should take you home and then go on ahead without you."

She felt even more embarrassed than before. How had she forgotten to leave her parents a note? He was right and she was wrong—but she wasn't about to admit that to him.

"They're my parents," she said. "I'll deal with them as I see fit—and I don't want to go home. Obadiah is a threat to me and my family."

He took the bridle of her horse and pulled her to a stop, storm clouds gathering in his gaze. "You are a young lady in my care. It is my duty to ensure that you and your reputation are left unhurt."

"What do you care for my reputation?" she asked, feeling her anger rise to the surface. "What do you care for me at all?"

Gideon frowned, his face softening. "I care a great deal. More than you might realize."

Tears threatened to spill from her eyes, so she looked away from him. She knew she was being ridiculous. Knew that the lack of sleep affected her mood and her thoughts. But she was hurt from the night before and she needed to release the pain.

"Hannie," Gideon said, taking her hand and tugging on it until she would look at him again. "What's wrong?"

"Wrong?" She wiped at her traitorous tears with her free hand, ready to throw all caution aside and speak plainly. "Why did you turn away from me last night?"

Her words appeared to slay him. His frown turned to a look of compassion and regret, though he did not let go of her hand. They were both wearing riding gloves, but she could still feel the heat from his skin through the leather.

"I knew if I didn't pull away, I would kiss you."

Hannie's pulse picked up and her breath stilled. So she hadn't been imagining the look in his eyes or the attraction between them. She leaned toward him, wanting nothing to hinder the words they needed to speak. "I would have welcomed your kiss."

He studied her, sadness and hope mingling in his gaze. "Everything is happening so quickly. A week ago, I didn't even know you."

"Can you deny this attraction we have for one another? Or the fact that our parents desire a match?"

Gideon shook his head. "But are those reasons to make decisions that will affect the rest of our lives? My greatest fear is that I would disappoint you."

A soft smile turned up her lips. "I am not afraid of disappointing you—because I know I will. How could I not? I'm human and fallible. I would never seek to hurt or disappoint, but I'm almost certain I will at some point—and so will you."

"Perhaps that is the greatest difference between us. You are fine with that thought, whereas it frightens me more than almost anything else."

There was nothing Hannie could say to change his mind—nor would she even try. She loved Gideon but would never force him to marry her. If they were to be husband and wife, he would have to come to her without a single reservation. There was no other way.

Hannie pulled her hand from his and tapped the side of her mare to start trotting again.

"Shouldn't we turn back?" he asked as he caught up to her for the second time. "Your parents will be sick with worry."

"We're halfway there," she said, feeling a sudden burst of energy to complete the trip. "Whether we go back now or in a few hours, my parents will be angry. We might as well finish the job we started."

They rode for several minutes before Gideon said, "Hannie, I want you to know I care for you. I just don't—"

"Until you do," she said, keeping her gaze straight ahead, "you don't need to say another word about it."

It was the only way she knew to maintain a bit of dignity while her emotions were running amok.

Gideon knew he was a fool. Hannie Van Brunt cared for him—perhaps loved him. She was beautiful, smart, determined, and devoted. Her father was probably the wealthiest man in upstate New York, and she would inherit it all.

Besides all that, he loved her. And even when she drove him to distraction with her stubbornness, he still wanted to hold her in his arms and spend every waking minute with her. He admired her spunk and her ability to speak openly and freely, despite everything.

So then, why did he hesitate? Why did he not tell her how he was feeling?

Other than the fact that he'd known her less than a week?

The landscape opened up, revealing Long Island Sound to their right. It gave Gideon a magnificent view of the vast sky. Off to the west, a line of clouds hovered low and menacing against the horizon. If they were lucky, the storm would shift and miss them. As it was, they were already guaranteed a storm when they arrived back at the Van Brunt home. Brom would be furious, and rightfully so. He would blame Gideon, who should have been a gentleman and said no to Hannie. He would be mad at Hannie too, since she knew better than to run off without leaving word.

But none of that mattered right now. All that mattered was this moment and the pain he had caused. He had managed to hurt Hannie, and there was little he could do to fix it. He wanted to be sure that their futures aligned before he told her he loved her. It was the right thing to do. But how long might that take? Was he like Brom, knowing in five minutes that his love for Hannie would not change, even if God allowed them fifty years together?

"We don't have far to go," Hannie said. "Greenwich is only another mile or two on the shores of Long Island Sound."

Gideon was thankful for that. He wanted to shift his attention to something else right now.

They rode until they came into town. It was a pretty little village with a small harbor, much like North Tarrytown on the Hudson River. The boat traffic was high on the sound, and it appeared that today was market day with wagons filled with produce lining the main street.

"Where should we begin?" Hannie asked Gideon.

The town wasn't overly large, but it was still a daunting prospect. It had been at least thirty years since Ichabod had left Greenwich, if not longer. There might not be anyone in town who even knew the family. "Let's start at the first tavern we see. The locals usually frequent such places, and we might have some luck there. I could also use some refreshment."

Hannie nodded, her gaze roaming the road as if she were searching for Ichabod himself, though she wouldn't know what he looked like.

It didn't take them long to find the Bosworth Tavern. It was a two-story building with third-floor dormer windows overlooking the sound. Tall, brick chimneys flanked both ends and a wide porch welcomed guests. Several men were entering the building, while half a dozen horses were tethered out front. It looked busy and well used, a good sign for their purposes.

They dismounted their horses and wrapped their reins around the hitching post near a watering trough. Gideon was stiff and sore from two and a half hours in the saddle. The horses were tired and in need of water. They had pushed them to get to Greenwich as quickly as possible, and all of them were showing the effects of their traveling.

Hannie moved slowly up the steps, appearing to feel as sore as he was.

He opened the front door for her, and they entered the cool, dark interior. The main room was long, low, and wide. Several tables were already filled by patrons who looked up at them as they walked through the front door.

"Whom should we question?" Hannie asked as they took a seat at the first available table.

"Perhaps the serving girl."

As he spoke, the young woman approached their table.

"What will you have?" she asked.

"Some cider, please," Gideon said, looking at Hannie with a question in his gaze. When she nodded, he said, "For both of us."

The servant began to turn away, but Gideon said, "We are looking for someone, and we were wondering if you might be able to help us."

"Who might you be seeking?"

"We are looking for the family named Crane. Perhaps a Mrs. Crane, mother of a man named Ichabod."

"You mean, the Cranes from the story?"

Gideon sat up a little straighter. "Do you know 'The Legend of Sleepy Hollow'?"

"Aye. And I know who you be looking for. Ichabod's sister, Penelope Crane, still lives in the old family home on Elizabeth's Point." She motioned to the door they'd just entered. "Just down the road at the end of the street. It's a blue house with dark blue shutters. Everyone knows her, though she hardly leaves her house, especially since the story was published. Too many people stop her to ask questions, but she likes to keep to herself. A strange woman, she is."

"Thank you." Gideon couldn't believe it had been that easy. He looked to Hannie, shaking his head in wonder. "Your feelings have been correct. First, the attic at Hans Van Ripper's home, and now here."

Hannie smiled, though it was easy to see she was tired and thirsty. "I knew we'd find something."

They drank their cider as quickly as they could and left the tavern. Since they were close, they didn't mount their horses, but led them by the reins down the street until they came to the blue house.

Gideon took a deep breath. "Are you ready?"

"If this means we can be done with Obadiah, I would face the whole British army. One strange woman is nothing."

He chuckled as they tethered the horses to the picket fence.

Hannie ran her hands down her gown. It was wrinkled and travel-worn, but she still looked beautiful. She walked up the cobble path to the front door, her head held high. She exuded confidence, and though he knew she must be uneasy approaching a stranger in an unfamiliar town, she didn't show any fear. It was yet one more thing for him to admire.

With just as much determination as Hannie gave to everything else, she lifted the brass knocker on the door and rapped it a few times before stepping back.

"I'm proud of you," Gideon said to her. "Your pluck is contagious and admirable."

She tossed him a look, her blue eyes sparking. "I'm desperate to clear Papa's name and be rid of Obadiah. I have no choice but to be plucky."

"You do have a choice," he reminded her. "You could be at home, following your parents' wishes. It would be safer."

A slow, sheepish smile tilted her lips. "Safer, but would it be as fun?"

They waited for several minutes, and Hannie knocked once again.

"What if she's not at home?" she finally asked.

"Then we'll wait as long as it takes."

Hannie cast her glance up at the sky, as if trying to determine the time—or looking at the oncoming storm. It was probably nine o'clock by now. If they could leave by ten, they might be home by one. They wouldn't be able to push their horses as fast this time. No doubt her parents would be infuriated with her absence, but hopefully they would be quick to forgive—or, at least, understand.

Finally, the door creaked open, and an older woman appeared, wearing a black gown. She peeked through the small crack. "Yes? May I help you?"

"I'm Hannie Van Brunt and this is Mr. Webb. We've come to ask you about your brother, Ichabod Crane."

"I do not talk about Ichabod to anyone. The story isn't true. Leave me alone." She started to close the door again, but Hannie lifted her hand.

"Please," she said, her voice desperate. "My father is Abraham Van Brunt—Brom Bones from 'The Legend of Sleepy Hollow.' I'm not here to discuss the book. I'm here about Ichabod."

Miss Crane stopped closing the door and narrowed her eyes at Hannie. "Your father is Brom Bones?"

"Yes. Can we please talk with you? My father has been accused of killing Ichabod, but I know it's not true. Ichabod left Sleepy Hollow the night my father frightened him. All I need to know is where he went."

A long pause followed Hannie's plea as Miss Crane studied her. Deep wrinkles lined her face. She was tall and slim, like Obadiah, and had the same hawk-like nose. Her gray hair was in a tight bun and her skin was pale, as if she rarely saw the light of day.

in Sleepy Hollow, New York

"Who accused your father of killing Ichabod?" Miss Crane finally asked. "Especially after all these years?"

Hannie let out a breath, as if she was relieved that Miss Crane would speak to her.

"My father was accused by your other brother, Obadiah."

Miss Crane frowned and opened the door a little wider. "What did you say?"

"I said that Obadiah accused Papa."

There was another pause, and then Miss Crane said, "I don't have a brother named Obadiah."

Chapter Eight

Hannie stared at Miss Crane, confused by what she had just heard. "You don't have a brother named Obadiah Crane? Then who is the man in Sleepy Hollow accusing my father of murdering Ichabod?"

Miss Crane let out a loud sigh and opened the door a little farther. "You might as well come inside."

The door creaked from unuse as Miss Crane took a step back. A stale smell emanated from the house, mingling with the scent of spices and lemon polish.

Gideon motioned for Hannie to precede him. As she walked over the threshold, she took note of the beautiful trim and intricate wood detailing on the stair railing. The interior of the house looked as if time had stood still. A tall grandfather clock chimed nine times, indicating the hour.

"Have a seat in the parlor," Miss Crane said. "I wasn't expecting you, so I don't have any refreshments."

"We're not in need of anything," Hannie reassured her. "Just some information."

Hannie still wasn't sure what Miss Crane meant about not having a brother named Obadiah. Was Obadiah dead? Or had he never existed?

The furniture in the parlor was in pristine shape. It was also very old—perhaps as old as Greenwich itself. Hannie took a seat on the stiff sofa, and Gideon sat beside her. She felt safer knowing he was close at hand. He gave her a sense of strength and confidence she'd never felt before. She wasn't even sure she could have come to Greenwich without him.

Miss Crane took a seat on a chair next to the sofa and set her cane aside.

Hannie wasn't sure if she should begin the conversation or if she should wait for her hostess.

The silence dragged on, so Hannie finally asked, "What do you mean, you don't have a brother named Obadiah?"

"What could I mean, Miss Van Brunt? I do not, nor have I ever, had a brother named Obadiah."

"Then who is in Sleepy Hollow?" Gideon asked.

Miss Crane folded her hands in her lap. "I fear I know the answer, though I do not know why he would do such a thing."

"Who is he?" Hannie sat forward on the sofa, her heart pounding as she waited for Miss Crane's answer.

"I believe," Miss Crane said, raising one eyebrow, "that the man who is in Sleepy Hollow, accusing your father of murder, is Ichabod himself."

"Ichabod?" Hannie frowned. "So he's not dead?"

"No, at least not since he last wrote to me about six weeks ago." Miss Crane used her cane to pull herself to her feet again. She slowly moved to a secretary desk along the wall and opened the cover. A stack of envelopes was tucked into one of the cubbies. She removed them and brought them to Hannie.

"As you can see, my brother was not murdered thirty-one years ago, but moved to Pittsburgh, Pennsylvania, and became a schoolmaster there."

Hannie took the letters. "May I open one?"

"You may." Miss Crane resumed her seat on the chair. "I saw him once, in all these years. After he left Sleepy Hollow, he returned here to Greenwich, quite despondent. My mother was still alive at the time. He did not tell us why his job ended in Sleepy Hollow, just that it had. He was morose and melancholy for several months, and my mother encouraged him to find another place of employment as soon as possible to rally his spirits."

"And that's when he went to Pennsylvania?" Hannie asked, opening the first letter on the stack—the most recent one.

"Yes. He wrote about once a month, all these years, so I know he did not die in Sleepy Hollow."

"Did he marry?" Gideon asked.

"No." Miss Crane shook her head. "I believe Ichabod fell in love while he was in Sleepy Hollow, and he never forgot about the young lady. It wasn't until the story came out that I knew her name."

"Katrina Van Tassel," Hannie said. "My mother."

"I believe so." Miss Crane laid her hands on the armrests. "I don't know what attraction Katrina held over my brother, but it was powerful."

Hannie suspected it was more than her mother that held sway over Ichabod. The land was a tempting prospect for any man.

Any man except Gideon, apparently.

She wouldn't let herself think about that right now. There were more important things to discuss today.

"Why do you think Ichabod is in Sleepy Hollow, pretending to be Obadiah?" Gideon asked.

The answer stared Hannie in the face.

in Sleepy Hollow, New York

"He mentioned something about it in his last letter," Hannie said, showing it to Gideon.

It took Gideon a couple of moments before he found the paragraph that had stood out to Hannie, and he read it aloud. "Mr. Irving's book has made a mockery of me. What happened in Sleepy Hollow has always been an embarrassment, but only I and a few people in New York knew what happened. Now, the whole world knows, and Brom Bones is to blame. I will make him wish he never played that trick on me or shared the story with Mr. Irving in the first place."

"The handwriting looks like it matches the letter I received last night from Obadiah—or rather Ichabod," Hannie said, wishing she had saved it to compare.

Gideon reached into his pocket and pulled out a piece of paper. It was wrinkled, though it looked like he had tried to smooth it out again before folding it into a square. He opened it then held it up to compare the handwriting. It matched perfectly.

Relief filled Hannie. Her father would not be convicted of murder. They knew who Obadiah was, and they had the evidence that he had plans to destroy Papa's life.

"May we take this letter with us?" Hannie asked Miss Crane. "I would like proof that Ichabod is alive and that he wants to make Papa pay for his embarrassment."

Miss Crane lifted her chin. "He is my brother."

Hannie stared at the older woman for a moment. What did she mean? Would she not let them take the letter?

Thankfully, Miss Crane continued. "I do not wish to aid you in proving he is guilty of making a false accusation."

"But—"

Miss Crane held up her hand. "He was the victim thirty-one years ago when your father chose to chase him down the road with a pumpkin. However, he is no longer the victim. What he wants is to destroy an entire family. His punishment for your father does not match the original crime committed. He should be held accountable for what he has done."

"Does that mean we can take the letter?" Hannie asked, breathless as she waited for the answer.

"Yes. Please take any letters you think would help you."

"I don't believe we'll need anything else," Hannie said. "If the sheriff has any questions, can he come here and speak to you?"

Miss Crane closed her eyes briefly, as if Hannie asked of her the hardest sacrifice of all.

"*If* he needs to talk to me, then yes, I will let him in. But please, tell him I'd rather not speak to anyone."

"I believe we have everything we need," Gideon said. "We don't want to take up more of your time. We should be heading back to Sleepy Hollow as soon as possible."

Miss Crane began to rise from her spot on the chair, appearing eager to see them gone.

"Thank you for all your help," Hannie said to her. "I'm so happy we found you."

The trio walked to the foyer together and Miss Crane opened the front door. As Gideon motioned for Hannie to precede him, she turned and asked Miss Crane, "Is there anything you'd like me to say to your brother?"

She sighed. "He will be angry with me," she said. "Perhaps it's best if you didn't."

Hannie nodded, wishing she could do more for Miss Crane, though she doubted the elderly woman wanted anything for her troubles.

Miss Crane closed the door behind them without a farewell, but Hannie didn't mind. They had the letter, and they had the information they needed to clear her father's name. That was all that mattered.

"I don't like the look of that storm," Gideon said as they walked to the front gate.

Hannie's gaze went to the western sky. The clouds had moved closer, but they were still a ways off. "How long do you think it will take for the storm to get here?"

"There's no way of knowing. And," he added as he untied the reins of his horse, "it could shift course and not hit us at all."

"We cannot wait it out. It could be hours, and we need to be home as soon as possible." She took the reins of her horse but looked to Gideon to see what he wanted to do.

He shook his head. "I don't like either option before us. Either we leave now and pray we get back to Sleepy Hollow without getting hit by the storm, or we stay here and wait for it to pass."

"I think we should leave now and pray it doesn't overtake us." Even as she said it, her pulse skittered to think about being in the midst of an autumnal Northeast storm without protection. Storms in late October could be unpredictable, with the possibility of rain, hail, sleet, or even snow. As she looked at the sky again, she put Ichabod's letter into her saddlebag.

Gideon came to her side. "I hate to push the horses, since they are still tired from our ride here, but I don't think we have any choice."

Hannie nodded and allowed Gideon to help her mount her horse. The air had cooled considerably, but if the sky stayed clear, the sun would offer a bit of warmth for their trek back to Sleepy Hollow. She wore a thick jacket and a warm bonnet. It would have to be enough.

"I want to get back as soon as possible," she said. "Not only to put my parents' fears to rest, but to give this information to the sheriff."

Gideon mounted his horse as well and tugged on the reins to get the gelding to turn toward the west—and home. "Then let's be off. We'll pray for good weather."

Hannie nodded and tugged on her reins to follow Gideon's lead. She would pray with all her might.

For the first hour of their journey back to Sleepy Hollow, Hannie spoke with nervous excitement about what they had discovered in Greenwich. Gideon knew she was anxious about the oncoming storm and the confrontation they would need to have with Ichabod Crane when they arrived home. She filled the time and space with words, and he didn't mind.

It helped to ease his own fears and keep his mind off the obstacles before them.

He loved traveling with her. He'd spent the past ten years of his life wandering by himself and he hadn't realized, until now, how lonely he had been. What would it have been like to have Hannie by his side all those years? Experiencing and discovering the world together? She saw things from a different light, one he admired. His memories had been his alone—until he'd come to Sleepy Hollow. Now he was making memories with her. Someday, when they were older, they would be able to recall the details of this day together.

If Brom Bones didn't kick him out of the hollow first. And, since that was a very real possibility, Gideon wasn't thinking too much about the future. Instead, he tried to focus on the present.

The wall of clouds moved closer, making no attempt at veering to the north or to the south. He watched the sky carefully, pushing his horse as fast as he could go without risking injury to the animal.

It didn't feel fast enough.

"We're going to run right into it, aren't we?" Hannie asked Gideon as her gaze lifted to the heavens.

"I'm afraid so."

"We should start looking for shelter."

"I have been for the past twenty minutes."

They had passed small farming villages along the way, but nothing substantial that would have a tavern or public house. They were just entering the long tunnel of trees again, with no view of the surrounding landscape to look for a welcoming farm. If his memory served him correctly, they would travel in this dense forest for several miles before coming out on the other side.

"I wish I had been paying attention to this stretch of land earlier this morning," he said to Hannie as a gust of wind tore down the alley of trees, whipping at his coat and sending a shiver along his spine.

"It was dark," she reminded him.

"Are you familiar with this stretch of road?"

"Not very. I've only been on it a few times before."

"You don't know anyone who lives nearby?"

Hannie shook her head. "I wish I did."

"Let's keep going until we find something."

They continued on, pressing forward as the wind increased.

Gideon tried to hold the lapels of his jacket together, but it didn't seem to help. The temperature had dropped by several degrees. He prayed, unceasingly, for a place to take cover.

Neither he nor Hannie spoke. Even if they had wanted to, it would be difficult. The wind howled, pushing against their every step.

Finally, they came to the end of the tunnel of trees. To the left was wide-open space and to the right were more trees. The road was built on a small ridge, but Gideon could see no building.

The rain finally began. First, in large, cold droplets, hitting Gideon in the face. They still had an hour of riding ahead of them, but it would be impossible to continue if the weather grew even more foul.

They trudged forward, the rain coming faster and faster. It was shoved about by the roaring wind, and for a moment, Gideon felt as if they were making no progress.

"There!" Hannie said over the wind and rain.

She pointed to the left. An abandoned barn stood off in the distance, a tree growing through the roof. It didn't look watertight, but it had withstood the test of time and could probably provide protection from at least one more storm.

The rain was coming down so hard now, it was getting difficult to see the road. Hannie veered off in the direction of the barn, and

Gideon followed. He could no longer see the barn, but he knew it was there.

Beneath the horse's hooves, the ground had become wet and muddy. His horse slipped and slid down the embankment, and it took all of Gideon's strength to keep seated in his saddle.

How was Hannie staying in her sidesaddle?

He looked up to make sure she was safe, but at that moment, her horse slid so fast, Hannie was thrown. She rolled down the embankment and slammed into a tree trunk.

"Hannie!" Gideon yelled, his heart plummeting at the sight. He scrambled off his horse, slipping to his knees in the mud. It was so thick, he struggled to stand, but a fierce determination pulled him to his feet, and he ran toward her. His clothing was soaked, and the temperature had dropped again, making him shiver, but he didn't care. The only thing he could think about was getting to Hannie.

He'd never known such fear existed until this moment. Every muscle in his body clenched with terror. What if she was hurt? Or worse? What if she had hit her head and was killed? Terror seized him.

She didn't move as he came to a stop at her side.

The rain battered against her face, running in rivulets into her unbound hair. She looked so at peace—so calm.

Too calm.

"Hannie," Gideon said as he gathered her into his arms. "Hannie!"

Her face scrunched in pain and she moaned so softly, he almost didn't hear it.

"Thank God," he said as he pulled her closer, embracing her. He needed to get her to the shelter. She wasn't safe here.

Gideon lifted her into his arms and stood. They were close enough to the barn, so he decided to carry her. It would take longer to get her on the horse.

It took sheer determination and willpower to move through the mud to the barn.

Thankfully, the horses followed. There was no door on the structure, so he went inside without any trouble.

Now he could see the tree more clearly. It ran right up through the middle, holding the building upright. Rain dripped through the holes in the roof, but there was one corner that looked dry. Gideon carried Hannie there and laid her gently on the dirt floor, still holding her in his arms.

Her eyes fluttered open, and she blinked several times. "Did we make it to the barn?"

"Yes." He smiled, his relief so intense, he wanted to hug her tight—but didn't want to hurt her. "You were thrown off your horse, and I think you hit your head."

She lifted her hand to a spot just behind her ear and winced. When she pulled her hand away, there was blood on her glove.

"So it seems I have. Is the horse injured?"

"No." Gideon shook his head and indicated where the horses had come into the barn. "I think they are just as happy as we are to be out of the storm."

The barn was musty, but it didn't look like it was being occupied by any other creatures save a family of mice. From where Gideon and Hannie were sitting, they had a perfect view of the storm outside the open door. Sleet mixed with rain and wind.

"I'm so cold," Hannie said as she shivered.

"If I had a match, I would build you a fire."

"I have some in my saddlebag. I hope they didn't get wet."

Gideon removed her from his arms and then rose to get the matches. He gathered dry branches and leaves from the barn and brought them to where Hannie sat. There was plenty of ventilation, with both doors open on either end of the building and a large gaping hole in the center of the roof. He laid the kindling out and lit the match. It started immediately, offering them a bit of heat to warm themselves and dry off.

"Do you need something for your head?" he asked her.

"No. It's only a scratch, though it bled like it was much worse."

"Head wounds will do that." Gideon sat next to her. "May I look?"

She nodded and turned her head.

Gently, tenderly, he moved aside her hair. It was damp and curly, and impossibly thick. The pins had come loose, and her bonnet hung around her neck. For a moment, he just wanted to touch it, and nothing else. But he needed to make sure her cut wasn't serious.

Thankfully, it was just a scratch, as she had said.

"It will be sore for a few days," he said. "You had quite a tumble."

She faced him, and he realized how close they were sitting. Her eyes were so blue and so beautiful, her skin soft and a bit pale. But it was her lips, bright red from the cold and the excitement, that drew his attention.

"It could be hours before the storm passes," she said quietly.

He wanted to kiss her—knew she wanted it too. "I don't think I was ever so scared in my life as I was the moment you were thrown from your horse. For a moment, I thought I had lost you." He *had* thought he lost her, and he realized, with startling clarity, that he never wanted to lose Hannie Van Brunt. He loved her and knew his life would never be the same now that he had met her. Even if he left Sleepy Hollow, he could never forget her—nor did he want to. "Now that I know you're in this world," he said, a bit breathless, "I cannot imagine being away from you. I don't *want* to be away from you."

"What are you saying, Gideon?"

"I love you, Hannie, and I'm sorry you had to get hurt for me to realize how very much."

A gentle smile lifted her lips. "I suppose it was worth it then."

"I know we haven't known each other long," he said, his excitement mounting. "But that's the fun part. I get to spend the rest of my life getting to know you."

Her smile didn't waver as her eyes lit up with joy. Yet—she hadn't said she loved him. Fear captured him again. What if she didn't return his feelings?

Slowly, she took off her gloves and placed her cool hands on either side of his face. "I can see the fear in your eyes."

Could she? Did she know him so well already?

"You have nothing to fear." Her hands felt feather-soft on his skin. "I love you too, Gideon Webb."

"Do you?"

She nodded. "I always knew that when I found the man with whom I wanted to spend my life, it would hit me like a thunderclap and I would know, with certainty, almost immediately. You are everything I've ever wanted, and nothing I expected."

He laughed as he laid his forehead against hers. "I didn't know what I wanted until I met you. Now I want nothing else."

Slowly, Gideon lowered his mouth to hers, savoring the moment their lips met. The kiss was sweet and soft, belying the storm that raged around them. He didn't want to hurt her injured head, so he pulled back before it grew deeper, as he knew it would.

"There's still the matter of your father," he said. "This storm will delay us further, and he will not be happy with me."

"Hopefully, with the evidence we've brought back with us, he'll overlook our disappearance."

"I pray you're right, because I need to ask him if he'll allow me to marry you. And a man does not want to ask a question like that to an angry father."

"You want to marry me?" Hannie whispered, awe in her gaze.

"Of course I do," he said, placing another kiss on her lips. "If you'll have me."

She ran her thumb over the curve of his cheek. "I will."

Chapter Nine

It was hard to know how much time passed before the storm cleared. Hannie was eager to be on their way, yet she had no wish to leave the warmth of Gideon's arms. He sat behind her, and she leaned against him, enjoying the heat from the fire and watching the storm rage. While he held her, they talked about the future. Gideon longed to pursue his dream to be a successful author. He told Hannie about some of the stories he had written, and he promised to let her read them when they returned home. She told him he needed to keep writing, no matter what, and she would do everything in her power to make sure he did.

She longed to be a mother one day and hoped to have a houseful of children. Though she was content to stay at the farm, she told him she would go wherever he wanted to go, and she meant it. She'd spent twenty-four years in one place, and she was now ready to see more of the world—as long as Gideon was by her side.

They both agreed that they wouldn't make any decisions until they spoke to her parents, and neither one brought up the fact that her father might not want to see them married, after all. Especially as the day lengthened and they had no idea how long it might be before they could head back to Sleepy Hollow.

When the storm finally dissipated, their clothes were dry and they were ready to be back on the road. It had grown late, and twilight was upon them.

"If we're fortunate," Hannie said, "the horses will be rested enough, and we'll be able to get back to Sleepy Hollow before it gets too dark."

Her head was pounding, though she would never admit it to Gideon. He was still worried about her, and she didn't want to trouble him overmuch. She had been able to braid her hair and tie off the end with a scrap of string from her saddlebag. After fastening her bonnet in place, she was ready to face the ride back home.

The ground was still muddy as they trudged out of the barn after making sure the last of the fire had been snuffed out. It took much longer than she hoped to get back to the main road. Climbing the embankment was treacherous, and she didn't want another accident.

Finally, they were on the road and the horses were able to pick up speed.

Neither one spoke as they pushed on for home. It took over an hour to reach the outskirts of Tarrytown. Moonlight danced upon the road, casting shadows and creating misshapen images amongst the trees. Stars peeked out from the drifting clouds, giving the whole landscape an eerie glow.

A shiver ran up Hannie's spine as the wind whispered secrets and the rustling of the leaves told tales. When a branch ran its icy fingers against her cheek, she cried out, drawing Gideon's attention.

"Is something wrong?" he asked.

"No." She shook her head, causing it to pound even more. "Just a branch."

He drew his horse closer to hers as they plodded along the empty road.

Whether they had intended to or not, they began to move slower. The horses were tired from a long day, and Hannie didn't want to draw too much attention as they made their way home. The last thing they needed were town gossips spreading rumors about the late-night ride.

A bullfrog lamented from a nearby marsh, startling Hannie. It was late and dark, and despite having Gideon at her side, her mind began to roam over the mystical stories of her youth. Ever since she was small, she had heard the spirited tales and been told wild and wonderful legends. For the most part, she had taken them in stride. There were stories about mourning sounds echoing from the graveyard at the Old Dutch Church in the vicinity of Major Andre's grave, and sightings of a woman in white that haunted the dark glen at Raven Rock. She was said to screech before a winter storm, warning everyone to take shelter, since she died at Raven Rock in the snow. But it was the story of the Headless Horseman who patrolled the country roads around the anniversary of his death, tethering his horse at night among the gravestones, that filled her mind with terror at the moment. It was silly, and she knew better. The legend was just make-believe, a tale that had been told over and over again, until it was so fantastical, it almost didn't resemble the first telling.

She'd heard her own father's tales often enough to know this to be true.

Nevertheless, as they moved along the dark road, she couldn't wait until they had passed the Old Dutch Church, sitting on a knoll above the creek. The wooden bridge nearby was old and rickety and shaded by large trees that blocked out the sun by day and the moon at night. Once she passed the church, she knew her imagination would settle, and she could focus on the conversation she was sure to have with her parents.

The sound of hooves behind them made Hannie's heart thump with terror. She turned—but there was no one on the road. Just wind and dark shadows.

"Did you hear that?" she asked Gideon.

He shook his head and looked behind them. "Perhaps it was the wind you heard."

Perhaps it was.

She tapped her horse's flanks, hoping to move faster.

They passed over several bridges along the route into Tarrytown. The village was quiet as they plodded through, though lights could be seen from windows. The earth was still soaked from the storm, and it didn't appear that anyone wanted to be outside. Smoke rose from chimneys, spiraling into the moonlit night, enveloping Hannie in the comforts of its smell. She wished they were near the hearth at home, warm and toasty. She didn't enjoy riding her horse at night, even in the best of circumstances.

Tarrytown was soon behind them and they were on their way into North Tarrytown. It was a much smaller village, with even fewer homes and people.

The sky grew darker and the shadows more ominous. Trees took on the shapes of men and monsters, and bushes looked like marauders, ready to pounce.

Hannie said nothing but prodded her horse to move faster, causing Gideon to hurry to keep up with her.

A dark, misshapen shadow sat on the edge of the road, near a familiar marsh. Hannie could not remember a tree being in that spot, though it sat perfectly still. She told herself she was mistaken, that there *was* a tree in that location. Though this one didn't look like a tree. It was different—lifelike. It seemed made of darkness, like a gigantic beast ready to spring upon them as soon as they were close enough.

She held her breath, hoping and praying it would turn out to be another tree or bush, or some other explainable object. Part of her wanted to point it out to Gideon, so he was aware and alert, but her rational mind knew it was foolish. She was being ridiculous and had let her imagination get the best of her.

They moved closer to the marsh, and Hannie kept her gaze glued to the object. Watching, waiting, hoping it was nothing.

Just as they were about to pass, the shadow moved.

Hannie's pulse leapt, causing her head to pound as the form shifted and scrambled upon the road. It was a rider on horseback, waiting in the shadows.

Visions of the Headless Horseman collided with the shadowy figure. It began to trot just behind them, nudging Hannie's horse to move faster.

"Who are you?" Gideon called into the darkness.

The rider did not answer.

"Who are you?" Gideon called again, but the only response was the snort of the stranger's horse.

Perhaps he was a local boy, hoping to play a prank, but whoever he was, Hannie had no wish for him to join them.

in Sleepy Hollow, New York

The rider began to gain on them, pulling closer to Hannie's side.

She kicked the flanks of her mare to start racing toward the church.

The moment the rider pulled abreast with her, the hair on the back of her head rose at the sight. He held a pumpkin in his hand—and he was raising it, as if to throw it at her.

Gideon saw the pumpkin as the rider raised it in his hand. It was massive and could easily unseat Hannie once again, causing even more damage. They were riding so fast, he wondered how she stayed seated. All these thoughts flashed through his mind as he reached out and captured the bridle of her horse, pulling it back.

The horses reared as the pumpkin went hurtling through space, missing both Hannie and Gideon.

She grabbed the horse's neck and held on for dear life until it came back down on all four feet.

Shards of pumpkin littered the road as the rider reared his own horse and turned back to face them.

"Ride home as fast as you can," Gideon said to Hannie. "I will confront the horseman."

"I cannot leave you." Her eyes were wide in the moonlight.

"Go, Hannie. I don't want you to get hurt."

He hit the rump of her mare, sending it off toward home. She passed the rider, who stopped his horse and looked from her to Gideon, as if he didn't know which one to chase.

Who was this madman? And why had he chosen to accost them on the road? Gideon knew all about the Headless Horseman stories, but he didn't believe any of them. He knew this was simply a man, looking to scare them. But why?

As the rider started to make his way back to Gideon, he knew he had only two choices: to outride him, or to confront him on the ground. Hannie had enough of a head start, and he didn't want her on the road by herself for long, so he decided to try and outride the assailant. If it was someone looking to pull a prank, he'd soon tire of the chase and stop to play the trick on the next unsuspecting traveler.

Gideon could no longer see Hannie on the dark road. As the rider was almost upon him, Gideon kicked the flanks of his horse and dashed toward the church. He crouched low on the gelding, hoping that Hannie was so far ahead they would not overtake her.

The rider must have turned, because Gideon heard him coming up from behind. His horse was fast, and it would not be long until he would outrun Gideon.

They raced through North Tarrytown, kicking up mud along the village's main road, and still the horseman pursued him. Gideon's heart pumped as fast as the hooves were pounding the ground. The wooden bridge by the Old Dutch Church drew closer, though it was hard to see in the darkness of night. On and on the horses galloped, and Gideon could not shake the story of the Headless Horseman from his thoughts.

Finally, Gideon passed over the rattling wood bridge, though he did not expect his pursuer to vanish into thin air. He continued on, past the church and the graveyard.

He saw Hannie just ahead, and his heart leapt, knowing she would soon be in the path of the madman who pursued him. Gideon looked behind to see how close the horseman was—but saw nothing. The rider must have turned off before the bridge, disappearing from the road.

Gideon overcame Hannie and pulled his lathering horse to a stop.

Terror gripped her expression as she looked back at the road. "Is he gone?"

"I think he turned off before the bridge."

"Do you think he was the Headless Horseman?"

"No." Gideon shook his head decisively, breathless from the chase. "I do not believe such a being exists."

"Why would he chase us?"

"To scare us, perhaps?"

"If he had hit me with that pumpkin, I might have been thrown from my horse again—and killed."

He breathed deeply, the truth of her words troubling him. "We must get you safely home."

A movement near the church graveyard brought Gideon's head up. There, moving among the stones, was a man. His silhouette was dark against the bright moon, and if Gideon didn't know better, he would think it was an old man. He was thin with long legs and arms.

"I suspect I know who the horseman is," Gideon said to Hannie, pointing at the graveyard. "It can be none other than Ichabod Crane. Look how long and lank he is, and how slowly he moves."

She turned to look in the direction he indicated.

Ichabod's fine horse, no doubt one he rented or stole, was tethered to the cemetery gate.

"Do you think he intended to kill me?" Hannie asked.

"I have no idea what his intentions were." Gideon dismounted his horse. "But I will find out." He handed the reins to Hannie. "Wait here. If he doesn't have a weapon, I should have no trouble overpowering him."

"What if he does have a weapon?" she whispered with alarm.

"He is old and feeble. I think I can best him."

"The famous last words of Gideon Webb," Hannie muttered.

Gideon smiled and approached the hill leading up to the church graveyard.

Ichabod was easy to spot as he sat atop a gravestone, his hands on his knees, his head hanging low, breathing deeply. No doubt the chase had winded him too. Gideon was already recovered as he wound his way through the stones. Some were as old as the graveyard itself, cracked and weathered with age, while others looked fresh and new. The church was not overly large, but its whitewashed stone gleamed bright under the moonlight.

"What did you hope to accomplish, chasing us through town?" Gideon asked.

Ichabod was startled, and he jumped to his feet, putting his hands out as if to defend himself.

Gideon would not tell Ichabod that they knew who he was, or that they had met his sister. Not yet. He needed the element of surprise on his side. "Did you wish to hurt Hannie?"

"I only wished to scare you. Brom Bones and his entire family deserve to pay for the pain and humiliation they put my brother through."

"How did you know we were going to be on the road?"

"I saw you leave town this morning from the window of the inn. I knew which direction you had traveled and heard a rumor that you were missing. I deduced that if you came back tonight, you would return from the same direction." He sneered. "A lover's tryst, perhaps? Oh, how Brom will loathe you when you return his sweet daughter to his humble abode. I do believe the sheriff is at their farm even now. Perhaps I'll join you as you tarry forth, just so I can see Brom's face when he realizes his innocent daughter is not so innocent any longer."

Anger seethed through Gideon, and he balled his fists to attack the man for slandering Hannie's name.

Ichabod flinched, as if he knew Gideon was about to strike—yet Gideon would not give him the satisfaction. He wanted Ichabod to be at the Van Brunts' home, especially if the sheriff was there. It would be Ichabod who would be shocked to learn the truth about their mission today.

"Come, if you'd like," Gideon said to Ichabod. "You should be there."

"I believe I will."

Gideon returned to his horse and mounted it as quickly as he could.

"Ichabod will follow us to your house," he said quietly to Hannie.

"What if he tries to hurt us again?"

"We don't have far to go, and with the element of surprise wasted, I don't believe he could. Besides…" He leaned in closer to her so Ichabod wouldn't overhear him from where he mounted his own horse. "The sheriff is at your home, and it will be best if Ichabod is there to hear what we've discovered."

Hannie looked skeptical, but Gideon was certain he had made the best move.

Ichabod's true identity was about to be revealed.

Chapter Ten

The cold wind nipped at Hannie all the way home, and with Ichabod not far behind, she couldn't stop herself from shivering. Gideon rode close by her side, turning from time to time to check on Ichabod. The man did not swerve to the right or to the left, but continued to follow them along the road, up the drive, and to the front door of the Van Brunt home.

Lights filled the main floor of the house, spilling out onto the front porch and the side yard. Several carriages, wagons, and horses were waiting in the yard, telling Hannie there were people inside the house, waiting with her parents. Papa and Mama would be pacing the floor, her mother had probably baked for hours, and her father would be puffing on his pipe. They would be worried and furious, and they had every right to be. Especially when they saw how stained her dress was and how messy her hair. When they learned that she'd been thrown from a horse and hit her head, they'd be irate.

And most of that anger would be directed at Gideon.

But they would also be relieved that Hannie and Gideon had uncovered the truth about Ichabod Crane.

They brought their horses to a stop outside the front porch. Gideon leapt from his gelding and then helped Hannie dismount from her mare, keeping a watchful eye on Ichabod.

in Sleepy Hollow, New York

He lingered long enough to hand the horses off to the stable boy with instructions to give them plenty of food, water, and care. Then he and Hannie started up the stairs.

Ichabod did the same, not far behind them.

"No matter what happens," Gideon said to Hannie, "I will fight for you."

A tender smile found its way to her lips, despite everything they were about to face.

Hannie opened the front door and was immediately met with the smell of sweet baked goods and pipe smoke. Warmth was her next sensation as it wrapped around her and drew her over the threshold. She had never been more thankful for her home than at this moment.

"Hannie?" Her mother called out to her as she rushed out of the parlor and met Hannie in the front entrance. "Oh, my dear, dear daughter." She pulled Hannie into a tight embrace, jarring her head in her exuberance. Hannie winced but would not add more concern to this reunion by telling her mother about her accident right now. "Where have you been? And why do you look so frightful? As if you've been chased by wild banshees and tossed in the mud?"

Papa entered the foyer, a ring of smoke around his head. The sheriff was close on his heels, and her aunts, uncles, cousins, and even a few neighbors crowded around the archway to see and hear the reunion.

"Hannie," Papa said as he hugged her next, relief awash over his face.

Gideon and Ichabod entered the house at that moment, making everyone turn to see who else had arrived.

Papa pulled back from Hannie, and in an instant his relief was replaced with anger. His eyes snapped with it and his mouth curled.

"What do you have to say for yourself, Mr. Webb? Bringing my daughter back to us, looking this way?"

"We have a lot to explain," Gideon said. "I know you're angry—"

"Angry does not begin to describe how I feel," Papa said. "And you *will* explain yourself. We were about to send out a search party." He looked at Ichabod, as if seeing him for the first time. "And you! What are you doing in this house? You were told to never return."

Ichabod looked as winded as Hannie felt. His hair was disheveled, his skin was pale and pasty, and he still struggled to breathe normally. "I came to see your family's downfall."

Papa moved toward Ichabod, as if to throw him out, but Hannie stepped in his way. "I want him here. We have something to tell you—all of you." Her legs were shaking uncontrollably. "Can we sit down in the parlor? I fear I will not be able to stand for long."

"Goodness," Mama said as she took Hannie by the elbow and led her into the parlor, pushing past the gawkers. "Make room for Hannie," she instructed the aunts.

Tante Gertrud, being the youngest, was cast off the sofa, allowing Hannie a place to sit. Tante Abigael patted Hannie's leg, as if Hannie were a victim, while simultaneously scowling at Gideon, who was not allowed to sit.

Ichabod and the sheriff followed them into the crowded room.

"I know I have disappointed and worried you," Hannie said as she looked to her mother and father. "But I have good reason. Today, Gideon and I left before dawn to ride to Greenwich."

The moment she said the name of the town, Ichabod took a step back, as if he meant to escape.

"Sheriff," Hannie said, "do not let Mr. Crane leave. He will be very interested to hear what we've discovered."

The sheriff latched onto Ichabod's arm and prevented him from leaving.

"Gideon and I discovered that Mr. Ichabod Crane originated in Greenwich, so we went there to locate his family," Hannie continued. "We were able to find his sister, who still lives in the family home on Elizabeth's Point."

Ichabod's nostrils flared and his eyes narrowed.

"Miss Crane informed us that she does not have a brother named Obadiah, and that Ichabod, in fact, did not die here in Sleepy Hollow, but took a job in Pittsburgh, Pennsylvania, where he has been living ever since."

A round of surprised exclamations filled the room.

"I have a letter in my possession, written to Miss Crane from Ichabod just six weeks ago, stating that he planned to take revenge on Papa for the humiliation caused him by Mr. Irving's story." Hannie felt pleased with herself. "The man before us is not Obadiah Crane, but Ichabod Crane, who has returned to make false accusations against my father."

"Is this true?" the sheriff asked Ichabod.

The man looked defeated, and there was no other defense he could give. "Brom didn't deserve any of the good fortunes he got," he said as he cast a glare at his nemesis. "You didn't deserve Katrina, or this farm, or your daughter. You don't deserve to be the hero of Mr. Irving's story—or any other story, for that matter. You were cruel when you tricked me that night, long ago, and you've made a laughingstock of me ever since."

Papa walked over to Ichabod and nodded. "You're right. What I did was cruel to you, and for that, I am truly sorry."

Ichabod stared at Papa for several moments and then said to the sheriff, "Take me away. I don't care where we go. I never want to see this house or these people ever again."

The sheriff obliged him, and they left the house.

"The party is over," Papa said to their family and friends. "Thank you for coming, but now that Hannie is home, there are things we need to discuss in private."

"Like a wedding date?" Tante Eva said with a chuckle. "A girl doesn't spend a day unchaperoned with a young man—and come home looking like she does—without a wedding soon afterward."

If Hannie and Gideon had come home unobserved, Tante Eva's words might not have rung true. But as it was, the entire family had witnessed their arrival, and their reputations would be ruined. Hannie hadn't considered that in her plans to clear her father's name.

Slowly, the family took their leave, and it was just Hannie and Gideon facing her parents.

"What do you have to say for yourself?" Papa asked Gideon.

Gideon stood beside Hannie, his head held high. "I love your daughter, and I'd like to marry her."

Mama took in a sharp inhale, and Papa looked a bit surprised, as if he hadn't expected that answer.

"I went with Hannie today because I knew if I didn't, she would undoubtedly go by herself," Gideon explained. "I knew you would not be pleased, but I also knew that she would not be deterred."

Papa cast a look at Mama, as if he had to agree.

"I tried my best to keep her safe," Gideon said, "but we were overtaken by the storm. We would have been home hours ago, but we took shelter and waited until it passed."

"Probably the wisest thing you did all day," Papa said, his anger starting to dissipate.

"I think the wisest thing I did today," Gideon continued, "was realize how much I love your daughter. I've asked her to be my wife, with your blessing, and I hope you'll offer it to us. I want to spend the rest of my life proving to Hannie that I am worthy of her love."

Hannie reached for his hand, her heart expanding at his words.

"Do you love this man?" Papa asked her.

"I do." Hannie nodded, tears coming to her eyes.

"Then I see no reason why we shouldn't plan a wedding." Papa smiled. "And the sooner the better."

Gideon turned his face to Hannie, love and joy in his gray eyes.

"The sooner the better," he said to her.

Hannie couldn't agree more.

***

The wedding day dawned bright and cold, the last weekend in November. Thankfully, the snow had held off, and the sky was a magnificent shade of blue. Most of the leaves had fallen from the trees, making them look stark against the landscape.

Gideon stood in the massive parlor of the Van Brunts' home, awaiting the sight of his bride-to-be. The house smelled of delicious foods, which Hannie and her mother had been preparing all week. The adjoining dining room was laden with the delicacies of a genuine Dutch-country feast. There were platters heaped with dozens of different cakes, donuts, and crullers, as well as apple pies, pumpkin pies, and peach pies. Beside those were plates of ham, smoked beef, and roasted chicken. Several dishes boasted preserved plums, peaches, and pears, and others of cream and milk. It was a scrumptious-looking meal that would feed the guests who had come from all over the countryside to celebrate this grand occasion—including Gideon's own father who had come from Massachusetts as soon as the engagement was announced.

It had been over a month since Gideon and Hannie had returned from Greenwich. Gideon had assumed his duties as the schoolmaster and had moved on to board at another house, closer to North Tarrytown. But every evening, when his work was done, he had come to the Van Brunts' to spend time with Hannie. In that month, he was more certain than ever that he wanted to make her his wife. Not only had he gotten to know her better, but he had spent time with Brom, learning about the farm. The two men had shared many conversations about the future, and they had come to an understanding.

As soon as the honeymoon trip to New York City was over, Gideon and Hannie would move into the small cottage Baltus Van Tassel had built for Brom and Katrina when they were married, thirty years ago. Gideon would work alongside Brom as a sort of apprentice. As Brom aged, he would assume less and less of the farm responsibilities, and Gideon would take over more. In a year or two, Gideon and Hannie would move into the mansion, and Brom and Katrina would return to the little cottage where they had started their marriage. They would be on hand to help with grandchildren, God willing, and Hannie and Gideon would be there to help them as they aged.

Gideon smiled, thinking about the plans they had made. He had never been more excited to establish roots and settle into a routine. His days would be spent working on the farm, and his nights would be devoted to Hannie and his writing. He'd already begun to compose a promising story. It was a tale of revenge and false identity, picking up thirty-one years after 'The Legend of Sleepy Hollow' finished. Gideon had never written something so effortlessly.

At that moment, Hannie appeared on her father's arm under the tall archway leading into the foyer. She looked radiant in a cream-colored gown with puffed sleeves and intricate pleats. Her face glowed with excitement and hope, especially when she met his gaze.

Gideon took a deep breath, his heart beating hard against his chest, and warmth filled every part of his being. Hannie had been made for him, and he for her. Her knew this with such certainty, it made him want to shout it from the rooftop. How had he deserved this kind of love and blessing? What had he done to garner God's favor?

The truth startled him.

He had done nothing. These gifts were from God, and they were simply that. Gifts.

A grin lifted his cheeks, and he knew he probably looked foolish, but he didn't care. He'd never been happier.

Brom walked Hannie down the aisle, between the family and friends who had gathered. They all stood since there were too many to bring chairs into the room.

His father was there, on one side, and Katrina stood on the other. She cried happy tears as she watched her daughter walk down the aisle. The handkerchief in her hand had been put to good use all day.

Finally, Hannie reached Gideon's side. When she looked at him, it was as if no one else was in the room with them. Her smile was sweet and a bit shy, her blue eyes shining.

"Who gives this woman to be married to this man?" the minister asked.

"Her mother and I," Brom said as he gently laid Hannie's hand into Gideon's. "I hope you will be very happy," he said to them.

Gideon would never remember what was said, or how long the ceremony lasted. All he would remember was Hannie at his side, calm—yet eager—as they shared their vows and made their commitment to each other.

When it was finally done, and the minister pronounced them husband and wife, Gideon and Hannie turned to the well-wishes of their family and friends.

A frolic would soon follow, with dancing, music, and all the food anyone could eat.

But the only thing Gideon could think about was being alone with Hannie—if just for a moment—so they could revel in the wonder of their marriage.

He took her hand and led her out of the parlor as the noise from everyone's voices echoed in his ears. Several people tried to stop them, but Gideon begged their forgiveness as he wove Hannie across the room.

Finally, they stepped into the hallway where several servants were bustling about, carrying more platters of food to the dining room. Gideon pushed open Brom's study door, knowing they were entering a forbidden place, but not caring much at the moment.

in Sleepy Hollow, New York

With a decided bang, Gideon closed the door behind Hannie and then pulled her into his arms. They were both breathless and laughing, but the moment they stood facing one another, their breathing stilled, and their laughter died on their lips.

They admired one another for a moment. Gideon could hardly believe she was his wife.

"Well," Gideon said finally. "How are you feeling, Mrs. Webb?"

She wrapped her arms around his neck, tugging his face down to hers. "I feel sublime, Mr. Webb."

Their lips met and they kissed for several minutes, rejoicing in the newness of their union.

"Do you think the others would mind if we left the party and went home to our little cottage?" Gideon asked.

"I think they'd mind a great deal." Hannie smiled. "Though I've never heard anything so tempting in my life."

He kissed her again, loving the feel of her in his arms. "I suppose we should stay—for a little while, anyway. Your mother has gone to so much trouble for us."

"She's loved every moment." Hannie finally pulled back and sighed. "If we don't return soon, someone will come looking for us."

A light knock at the door made both of them jump.

"May I come into my study?" Brom asked, a chuckle in his voice.

Gideon and Hannie moved away from the door as Brom entered.

"I hope you don't mind," Gideon said to his father-in-law. "We needed a little time alone."

"I don't mind at all," Brom said as he and Katrina entered the room. "If I remember our wedding day correctly, we left moments after the ceremony and didn't return until late that evening."

Katrina's cheeks turned pink at the mention.

Gideon stood with his arm around Hannie's waist. She laid her head against his chest, hugging her arms around him.

He never wanted her to leave his side again.

"Hannie, your mother and I wanted to speak to you two privately," Brom said, standing a little straighter. "We have a wedding gift for you."

"Another one?" Gideon asked. "You've already given us so much."

"This is a little different," Brom said.

Hannie lifted her head off Gideon's chest as she stood straight and faced her parents.

Brom handed Gideon an envelope. It was full of money.

"What is this?" Hannie asked, her eyes opening wide as she looked from the envelope to her parents.

"We want you to take an extended honeymoon," Katrina said. "Go wherever you want, for as long as you want. When you're ready to come back to the farm and settle down, we'll be here waiting. But until then, have some fun and explore the world."

The amount of money in the envelope was mind-boggling. Gideon was uncomfortable even holding it.

"Are you serious?" he asked the Van Brunts.

They looked at each other and smiled.

"We are very serious," Brom said. "Life will soon have you settled, hopefully with a passel of our grandchildren. So, be adventurous and take your time enjoying just the two of you for a while. Finish your novel. We'll be here, waiting for your return."

Gideon could hardly believe the gift they were offering to him and Hannie. When he looked at her, he saw she had tears in her eyes. She glanced up at him, her smile tremulous.

"Would you like to see the world, Hannie?" he asked her.

All she could do was nod as she wiped away her tears. She left Gideon's arms to hug her parents.

As they enfolded her in their embrace, Gideon could only marvel.

He'd finally found his story—and it had just begun.

Love Stirs the Pot

by
Ruth Logan Herne

He seldom, it is true, sent either his eyes or his thoughts beyond the boundaries of his own farm; but within those everything was snug, happy, and well-conditioned. He was satisfied with his wealth, but not proud of it; and piqued himself upon the hearty abundance, rather than the style in which he lived. His stronghold was situated on the banks of the Hudson, in one of those green, sheltered, fertile nooks in which the Dutch farmers are so fond of nestling. A great elm tree spread its broad branches over it, at the foot of which bubbled up a spring of the softest and sweetest water, in a little well formed of a barrel; and then stole sparkling away through the grass, to a neighboring brook, that babbled along among alders and dwarf willows.

From "The Legend of Sleepy Hollow"
by Washington Irving

Chapter One

Sleepy Hollow, New York
Present Day

Tess McIntosh couldn't help but think, as she stood whipping up a batch of White Mountain rolls in the kitchen of Granny June's Sleepy Hollow Soup Shop, that she was about as far removed from Lower Manhattan investment banking as a girl could get. And it didn't just feel nice. It felt great.

Tess closed the oven and checked the dough in the adjacent proofer. It wasn't quite ready, and she had just thirty-seven minutes until customers would start streaming through the thick tempered-glass front door facing Cortlandt Street. And Friday mornings were always busy.

Coffee time.

Gran's coffee was better than anything a big-name chain offered. Tess went through the swinging doors that separated the kitchen from the dining area.

A variety of warm scents simmered on the stove and soothed her soul—chicken noodle soup stock. Minestrone. Beef with barley, a fall favorite. It was too early for stews. Gran never made stews before November, and when she did, people stood in line to buy quarts of the rich, savory meal. Throw in a loaf of bread or a pack of fresh-made rolls, and you had a solid meal at an economical price.

Delectable.

Granny June specialized in feel-good food, using a mix of recipes as old as her nineteenth-century ancestors and as new as a click on her computer. And wafting through the air as customers made their delicious decisions was Gran's secret weapon: the enticing scent of baking bread.

Gran knew her business.

She knew how her upstate New York clientele loved their soup, and soup was an affordable restaurant commodity. Her business philosophy had never steered her wrong yet—give the people what they want, when they want it, at the best possible price, and they'll be yours forever.

Tess poured herself a cup of coffee then reached for the cream.

The back door slammed shut, and the front door opened.

She wasn't sure who was responsible for the former. But the latter? She recognized the face that stared at her. She remembered well that rugged stance and wide-eyed look that oozed innocence. Oh, she remembered him, all right. Remembered admiring him from a distance while he wooed her big sister, Bridget. He'd obviously never noticed Tess's schoolgirl crush as she watched from afar for over two long years.

He stared at her. Hard. As if trying to place her. Then she saw the light-bulb moment, that moment he finally put her face with a name. "Tess?" Did he really need to say it in the form of a question?

Ouch.

Double ouch when she added in that he'd only gotten better looking in the fourteen years since she'd last seen him. His romance with Bridget had dissolved, then he'd finished college and settled someplace upstate.

End of story.

Only now it seemed the story had a new chapter, and that was the last thing she expected.

Tess nodded. "Home to visit, Riley?" She kept her voice cool. Deliberately cool. An ice-factor of nine out of ten. And he deserved it, because if the big oaf didn't realize she'd been crushing on him all those years ago, shame on him.

"Kind of. Wow." His eyes widened. He gave her a smile—*that smile*—the one that had put her in gaga land years before. But she wasn't a lovestruck fifteen-year-old any longer. "Tess, you look great."

Flirt with him. Have some fun. That's what Bridget would do.

But she wasn't Bridget. She had no femme fatale skills, and maybe that's why her few romantic liaisons had dissolved before there was anything to write home about.

"You're helping Gran?" he asked.

A safe topic. Good. "I decided the latest financial debacle in Lower Manhattan was my last. I wanted tranquility."

"Can't get more tranquil than soup and bread," he replied.

Bread.

The rolls!

The timer hadn't gone off...because she hadn't set it. She'd intended to grab coffee and head straight back to the kitchen to form balls for the pull-apart rolls the customers loved—

She hurried to the kitchen.

Gran was there, leaning against the counter she used for dicing and slicing, and from the look on her face, Tess was in trouble. Big trouble.

The scent of scorched bread filled the air. Tess hurried to the oven and opened the door, magnifying the scent.

She grabbed potholders and quickly disposed of the rolls in the dumpster out back to minimize the noxious odor, then came back in.

Gran had tears in her eyes.

Gran rarely cried, and mostly when she was mad, and when she aimed her gaze at Tess, Gran was steaming. Tess hurried to her.

"I'm so sorry, Gran. I meant to set the timer. I know how quickly those rolls bake, and I'll be more careful. I promise. Cross my heart."

These rolls were persnickety. Customers liked their soft, chewy goodness. They weren't like a firm-crusted artisan bread, which gave a window of time.

Gran's White Mountain rolls were a town treasure, and she'd just ruined a tray of eighteen.

"Forget the rolls." Gran motioned Tess over.

She pointed a finger at the big butcher-block worktable in the center of the kitchen.

A full-color brochure lay open. It was filled with pictures of needy dogs and cats. Heart-wrenching photos. The kind that made people reach into their wallets. Next to it was an envelope marked *Return to Sender/Undeliverable*. Beneath it, a ten-dollar bill peeked out from the corner of a notecard written in Gran's familiar hand.

Tess looked from Gran to the brochure, confused.

"Gone." Gran folded her arms tight across her chest, as if choking on the words. "Gone. All of it. Except for this latest ten-dollar contribution I mailed last week."

She shook her head in dismay and repeated her lament. "Every cent is gone. The money collected for this fake shelter from so many folks around town. Dog lovers, like me. Cat lovers too. I was so sure this was a legitimate endeavor. I'd emailed back and forth with the so-called director of this rescue operation out near Elmira. He said he needed to raise funds to build a new shelter and expand their operations. He even promised a tour of their new facilities and a special weekend retreat come springtime for all those who invested over a thousand dollars to the cause. Said they would name a wing of the new center the Sleepy Hollow Haven if our town contributed enough. Some of us local animal lovers even had meetings about it, every Tuesday this summer until things got too busy." She bit back a sob.

Busy was an understatement for the tourism trade in the village of Sleepy Hollow, New York. The author Washington Irving had made the town famous two hundred years ago, and locals weren't afraid to cash in on it now. Tess moved closer. "Gran, I'm sorry."

"I'm the sorry one." Gran pulled off a sheet of paper towel, and when Tess offered her a tissue instead, Gran's lower lip stuck out, stubborn as ever. "I don't deserve soft tissues at the moment, Tess, although I appreciate the gesture. I have managed to unsuspectingly aid a scoundrel in bilking my friends and neighbors out of over twenty-one thousand dollars to help a cause that doesn't exist."

"How do you know it doesn't exist?" asked Riley, who had followed Tess into the kitchen. "Isn't it possible that this organization just has a small internet footprint? Or changed office addresses? Gran, there might be a reasonable explanation for all this. Let's check that out first, okay?"

June McIntosh wasn't Riley's grandmother, but half of Sleepy Hollow called her "Gran," and Riley had known her that way all his life.

"I did."

She spoke softly. As if she already knew the answer to his queries. And when Gran lifted her gaze to Riley's, Tess knew that was exactly the way it was.

"I checked, Riley. I checked the internet, I checked the banks, I did a cross-reference with names. Every account or address the foundation used is gone. Erased. Error codes popping up all over, showing this old gal the error of her ways. Well, let me tell you." Gran raised herself up to her full five-foot, two-inch height. "I don't go down easy. I don't go down without a fight. And I don't—"

Her right hand flailed. She raised it up, then brought it down quickly, clutching her heart.

And if Riley hadn't caught her as she crumpled, Granny June McIntosh would have toppled to the floor.

Riley O'Toole refused to think about what could have happened if he hadn't been there to catch their old family friend when she collapsed. But fortunately, he *was* there, at her request, and he was determined to figure out where the collected monies had gone. Gran wasn't alone in her love for animals. Sleepy Hollow and neighboring Tarrytown were home to a lot of pet lovers. Most of them were regular people, not the ones living in the new seven-figure-priced condos on the Hudson. "How's she doing?" he asked Tess when she finally came through the ER door several hours later.

"Okay." She looked shaken but in control, and he liked that. "The cardiologist said they're going to do a full battery of tests to see what interventions need to be done, but she—the cardiologist—said it looks mild, that no major damage was done to the heart, and a balloon procedure will set things right."

"I'm thanking God for that."

"Me too." The softness in her voice told him she was more affected by the incident than she wanted to let on. "I only just got back to town. I don't want my time with Gran to be over. Ever. Oh, Riley." She paused and touched his arm. She looked up at him, guilty. "I'm sorry. Gran told me about your dad. That was insensitive of me."

There was something nice about her touch, but it wasn't the feeling of her hand on his arm that took him by surprise.

It was her gaze. The heartfelt expression. The compassion. He'd had a lot of people share sympathies with him the last six months, but Tess's warmth spoke deeper. "It's a natural feeling, Tess. We're never really ready to say goodbye."

She gave his arm a light squeeze.

She didn't say anything more. No platitudes about Dad being in a better place, etc. He knew that. Believed it. But he still missed his father and wished he were here, running the shop and communing with boaters, fishermen, and sailors on top of teaching boating-safety courses for the state. Here to take the pressure off his mother. Here to make everything normal, once again.

But his father was gone, and Riley felt that hole in his heart every single day. He gestured to the door. "Are you staying? Or heading out?"

"Gran kicked me out. She said Marita couldn't handle the counter and the baking during a busy supper hour, especially in

October with so many fall visitors, so I'm on the clock. I can get things prepped for tomorrow…"

"And that way Gran isn't worrying about the restaurant while she's supposed to be resting and recovering."

"Exactly." They walked through the sliding glass doors together.

The weather had changed, not unusual for this time of year, but the cold wind and sharp rain showed a season in flux.

She glanced up at the sky, then him, then tugged the hood of her sweatshirt up over her head. "Thank you, Riley. Thanks for being there today." She sprinted across the ambulance lanes and raced for her car parked a block away. His was no closer, but as he watched her mad dash across the full parking lot, the urge to protect her from the rain swept over him.

Only he had nothing that would be of use. He wondered why that made him feel bad. It was just rain, right? Everyone got wet sometimes.

He didn't go home.

He went straight to Granny June's and pulled into one of the small parking spots behind the building. There were only six spots, and the old two-and-a-half-story structure had an apartment upstairs, a rental that gave Gran a solid monthly income. The apartment got two spots and the restaurant got the other four, which made parking a bear during busy times. Not impossible, if people didn't mind walking over a block from the open lot up the road or the church around the corner, but not easy in bad weather either.

Tess's car was on the road.

He'd passed it when he pulled in and he realized why as he turned into the back parking area.

Gran's car was taking up one of their assigned spots.

If Tess had parked here, someone else would have to roam the streets to hunt down a spot or park up the road. Instead, she'd done it.

He moved to the empty church lot, cut through the old schoolyard, and came into the prep kitchen through the back door.

Good smells surrounded him.

Enticing baskets of bread sat on the pass-through counter, and as he inhaled the heady aroma, Tess hurried into the kitchen.

She met his gaze.

He met hers. And then she said the words that made his heart beat a little stronger in his chest.

"I knew you'd come back."

He lifted a brow in question. She hadn't dashed home to get a dry shirt. She'd simply peeled off the hoodie and donned a baking smock instead, putting Gran first. "Because?"

"We've got a job to do." She pulled a tray of crusty bread out of the oven, set it down, and proceeded to brush each roll with soft butter. "A job we have to do together. Gran may have called you in for a consult without telling me about it, but there's no way I'm letting someone get away with this. Stealing money, misrepresenting fundraising, conning dollars from people who don't have extra, and putting my grandmother in the hospital. So, like it or not, I'm in, Riley. And I'm hoping you're okay with that, because, honestly"—she slanted a look up to him and it was her turn to arch a brow—"I can't in good conscience give you a choice in the matter."

Chapter Two

He didn't need a choice.

He realized that straight off. By the time they worked their way through a tourist-loaded early October weekend, he was pretty sure that his forensics internet technology job was a walk in the park compared with running a busy restaurant, even one with a limited menu like Granny June's.

The hospital planned to release Gran on Tuesday.

He showed up at Gran's house first thing Monday morning. They'd stayed late Sunday to do veggie prep for soup stock and dry-side measurements for the various breads. Marita would come in early to blend, knead, proof, and bake. That bought them a few hours. "I brought breakfast sandwiches and Diet Mountain Dew."

"How did you know I drink way too much of that stuff?" asked Tess.

"I could scare you by saying I stalked you on social media—"

"Except I avoid it, so I wouldn't fall for that particular ruse," she said as she unwrapped a sandwich. She inhaled and sighed. "This smells so good, Riley. Thank you. I don't think I've eaten much since Friday."

"Two rolls on Saturday and the cup of soup I pushed you to eat yesterday. But who's counting?" he teased. He waved his sandwich in the air. "This seemed healthier than cheese Danish, which you also love. Unless that's changed."

She looked puzzled for a moment. Then her forehead furrow eased. "You remember that from so long ago?"

"Part of what makes me good at what I do," he told her. He settled his laptop on the table but didn't open it. Instead, he moved to Gran's computer, set up on an old oak desk on the far side of the kitchen. "Do you know Gran's password?"

"She doesn't have one."

He rolled his eyes. "What is it with people ignoring cyber-security? Don't they realize how vulnerable they are?"

"You're talking three hundred and thirty million people in this country alone. I think most of us just play the odds." She had the grace to cringe slightly when he frowned. "But I'll make sure she does better. I had high-tech security for all my work on Wall Street, but I never thought a thing about it on my PC when I came here. Maybe it's a small-town thing? That makes me as guilty as Gran."

He transferred Gran's laptop to the table as he offered his reasoning for moving it. "Better light and much better seating."

Gran's little desk had an equally small chair drawn up alongside.

"The ice cream parlor chairs." Tess smiled. "I used to love sitting in those. She and Gramps bought two of them when that little custard shop sold out. Back when we were kids."

Riley grimaced in memory. "When the GM factory closed down. That made for tough times for a lot of people."

"It sure did. When I saw how dependent my dad was on that weekly paycheck, I knew I wanted to have a bigger say in my financial affairs."

Riley shot her a skeptical look. "You were seven, Tess."

"I like to think I was advanced for my age." She poured them both coffee and took the seat next to him so she could see the screen. "I saw how he worried. What it did to him. To their marriage." She made a face. "He was never the same after that. He tried. But it was different. And by the time the town was coming back to life when I was finishing high school, he was gone. Mom remarried and moved to Arizona. Bridget's in that really upscale part of Montana with her family, and Gran was here alone." She frowned. "That wasn't how I saw our future going. Too many greeting card commercials, I guess. The ones that show the whole family sitting around a big old table like this one while they're carving a turkey or the one with the soldier making coffee for the family on Christmas morning. That's the way I thought things would be."

He pulled up a computer folder labeled *All Creatures Pet Rescue*. He opened it, then whistled softly. "Gran made a spreadsheet?"

"I showed her how last year. She and the other donors wanted to keep track of how much they gave because of what the person said about naming a new wing after the town. We kept it simple."

"Well done. This is our witness list."

"Isn't it also our suspect list?"

Riley gave her a puzzled look. "This is an internet scam, Tess. It could be anyone from anywhere."

Tess stared at him. "I didn't even think to ask Gran where she sent her donations." Then her eyes grew wide. "But wait a minute—I brought Gran's things back here..."

She got up and left the room, coming back seconds later with an envelope in her hand. "Gran had her last donation sent back." She handed him the envelope. "The address is a post office box in Tarrytown."

Riley felt his heartrate speed up just a tick. "Excellent work, Tess. This really narrows the field for us. Now we can reasonably focus on someone close by—someone who might have a personal grudge against Gran or the soup shop."

"I don't suppose..." She looked at him hopefully.

He shook his head. "If her donation was returned, I think that would have to mean the box has been rented to someone else. Either it was returned to her right away, or the new person received this and turned it in to the postmaster, who sent it back to Gran."

"Gran feels so guilty about all this. I don't know how to make her feel better."

Riley shook his head. "All she did was offer an opportunity to donate. She didn't twist any arms. Did she?" he asked and added just enough surprise to his voice to make her smile. Everything felt better when Tess smiled, and if him being a little silly encouraged that, he'd do it more often.

"No, but that won't matter to her. You know how she is about neglected creatures. Human or fur-bearing."

"Mom said that Gran gives away almost as much soup as she sells. I'm guessing you help foot those meat and produce bills." He shoulder-nudged her as he pulled up Gran's email account. "It's a nice thing to do, Tess."

"It's not a big deal," she told him, then corrected herself. "Not big financially, to me personally. But to some of the people who live and work in Sleepy Hollow, it's clutch. Gran has a way of knowing who they are. She watches for those who fall through the cracks and then helps quietly. There are a lot of people who won't go to food pantries or shelters."

Should he confess that he was living in a million-dollar-plus home right now? The firm sublet the gorgeous townhouse for him when one of their executives was transferred overseas. It overlooked his parents' business and the mighty Hudson. Looking south he had the Manhattan skyline. Gazing north was the old lighthouse and the new upscale development on the old automaker's site. Normally he'd stay at his parents' house less than a mile away, but his sister's family was bunking there while their house was being renovated. Having two kids to run back and forth to Pocantico Hills school had helped keep Mom busy as the boating season drew to a close, but it also meant he needed another place to stay. Ichabod's Landing luxury townhomes became his current address by default. But if his brother-in-law accepted an out-of-state transfer, and his mom followed them to wherever that might lead, then this current chapter of his life would be over. And that felt wrong and weird all at once.

"There." Tess pointed to an email thread. "Check that out."

He clicked the latest email from allcreatures@helpthem.org and whistled softly when the page opened up. "Whoever did this knew how to tug the heartstrings, didn't he? Or she?"

"I'll say." The emails opened with a picture of a harshly treated animal, complete with name, age, and a gut-wrenching story. That was followed by an impassioned plea for monetary assistance.

But when Riley tried to email the account, an address-unfound notification came back almost instantly.

"Can you bust through a firewall?" asked Tess.

The request made him laugh. "Not if I want to keep my job, but there are ways to check things out without breaking laws. And one of the first ways is to check the donor list against the social media you avoid. You scope out whatever you can on Gran's accounts, and I'll see if I can track down where the donations were sent on the 'Fund Us Now' account." He slid Gran's laptop toward Tess and opened up his more sophisticated version.

Tess avoided social media purposely.

If there were people she wanted to see, she saw them. If she wanted to talk to them, she called them. Or texted them. She kept it simple for a couple of reasons.

People said too much on social media.

And she liked her privacy. She'd helped Gran set up the Sleepy Hollow Soup Shop's Facebook page years before, so when she opened up the page and saw over seven thousand likes, she was surprised and proud. The page was populated with comments from both tourists and locals. That meant a lot of people to check out.

"Did Gran use the soup shop Facebook site to seek out donations for the animals?" asked Riley.

Tess shook her head. "Not that I can see. There are links to a bunch of causes Gran supports. The church, the food pantry, and several others. The link to the website is there, but it's just one of a dozen others. No request for funds or special notice."

"See if she's given it a page," Riley suggested.

"I don't know what that means."

He got up and rounded the table. Then he put his arms around her from behind to look for additional pages.

He smelled wonderful.

Like soap and coffee and clean cotton wonderful, and it was all she could do to keep herself from leaning back, into that broad chest. She'd dreamed of that as a teen.

It seemed just as amazing now.

She didn't lean back though. She hunched forward slightly, gaining a much-needed inch and a half of space, and he still smelled downright amazing.

"There." He sighed softly, just enough for his breath to ruffle her hair. "She created two pages that are linked back to her page. Her personal page is this one." He showed her Granny June McIntosh's page. "Then the soup shop business page is linked from Gran's page, and she also set up a page for the foundation. Let's hide that one so no one else gets fooled."

He made the animal rescue site vanish with a few quick clicks. "I've archived it because we might need it for evidence. But this way no one will see it."

"But if it disappears, won't the thief realize Gran's on to him? Or her?"

"They're covering their tracks now. That means they were already worried or figured time might be drawing short, so they cut and ran—which we know from the returned mail. Do you have any pets, Tess?"

Tess shook her head. "No. I worked long hours. I knew people with pets in Manhattan, but it didn't fit my lifestyle. If I have a dog, I want time to be with my dog." She shrugged lightly as he eased away.

For just a moment—a too-brief moment—he let his hands rest on her shoulders, then he moved back to the other laptop.

She was being silly. She knew it. They were both here in the flux of change, and Tess didn't do romance casually.

You don't do much of anything casually, her brain scolded. *And you haven't done romance in a long time. Might want to rethink that one.*

She shoved the thought aside as she came across a tough comment on the soup shop's Facebook page. *"Stick to catering soup lunches. Don't you know there are literally hundreds of millions of humans going without in this world every single day? Why not help them? That's the thing to do, instead of these stupid cats running here, there, and everywhere, leaving paw prints on everyone's car."*

"Hey." She motioned Riley over. "What do you think of this? She's scolding Gran for helping pets."

Riley read the comment aloud. "She sounds frustrated," he agreed. "Susan Mary Andreas. Do you know her?"

Tess shook her head. "Nope." She entered the name in her phone. "But I intend to. Do you think someone would go to that extreme to teach Gran a lesson, Riley?"

"I think there are people that entrench themselves on both sides of the pet issue," he told her. "You have some that keep their pets indoors 24/7, and some that like their pets to live an indoor/outdoor life, and they rarely agree. I know this because I live between two of them outside of Rochester. I'm like the DMZ of Rockwood Landing."

"You're kidding."

He shook his head. "It's a thing, I guess. I don't have a pet yet." He frowned as he took a quick photo of Susan Mary's Facebook page. "Primarily because I don't want to hear the lecture from either one. But once I settle someplace that isn't between two bickering old women…"

"I don't think we can call people old anymore," she whispered to him, as if someone could hear her. "Age-advanced, maybe?"

He laughed, and it felt good to hear him laugh. "Clearly, I'm an insensitive clod. Anyway, once I'm in a place that I'm going to call home for a while, I'm getting a dog. Like Gwinner."

"I loved Gwinner." Gwinner was the golden retriever Riley's family had for years when they were all growing up. Carrie wanted to name the dog Goldie and Riley wanted to name her Winner, so they combined the two names to Gwinner. "How long has she been gone?"

"Nearly ten years now. My mom got a funny little dog after that. A corgi. He's cute, but he's getting on in years and she said she won't get another pet." He frowned as he said that.

"I wonder why." She tipped her gaze up to him.

He slanted his gaze down to hers, and there it was again. That connection. Like when a spark flies upward, making the moment significant.

"Says she's too old for a puppy and too busy to train one properly. I think she's still grieving," he continued. "The town is changing, her life has taken a huge left turn with Dad gone, and she's getting inquiries on the marina from developers. It was scrub property butting up to the auto plant when they bought it for the boats thirty-five years ago. Now it's prime and everyone and their brother wants it."

"Nice retirement fund," she said.

Riley didn't agree. "Except she's only sixty and has no plans to retire, even if she sells the boat business and the land. You know my mom."

She didn't, not really, and he realized that almost instantly. "Wait, you don't, do you? She likes working. Keeping busy. She's not the type to sit around and get old."

"Like Gran only ten years younger."

"Yes. I keep telling Mom not to make any big decisions for a while, but I can tell she's worried. Carrie's husband might be transferred out of state, so that's a big question mark right now. They're staying at Mom's while their kitchen is being remodeled, and that's like the best medicine at the moment. Mom loves her grandkids, and I can't imagine her staying here alone if they move away. And winter's a bear. You know that. There's not much to do, and it's going to be worse now that Dad's passed away. Having Carrie's family underfoot will get us through the holidays, but then the remodeling will be done, I'm scheduled to be back in Rochester, and Mom will be alone in the height of winter. Wait. Whoa." He double-clicked on something and motioned her over. "Hold that thought. I might have hit the jackpot."

"What've you got?"

He swung the screen her way. "They held a summer potluck to raise money for the rescue and someone did us the favor of labeling the pics. Looks like someone named Frances Lessing was the organizer."

"Is she in the pictures?"

"That would be too easy. But it shouldn't take long for us to hear something. There's something about missing money that loosens lips. No one wants to be accused, and they have the common goal of wanting their money found. Nobody likes being duped."

"I hate that Gran's going to be embarrassed." She drew a deep breath as she began a list of local names who'd attended the potluck. "But I know Gran, and she'd rather bear the shame than pretend nothing happened. There's not a dishonest bone in her body. I won't deny it feels really good to come back home to that."

"The city's a little different?"

She made a face at him, then laughed. "It's amazing how a forty-minute train ride can turn things upside down, isn't it? Then again, we've got all these new developments here, a lot of rich people moving in, and a part of me wonders how will the locals survive? How will they pay rent and taxes? I can't even imagine someone like Gran being able to buy a house here now. I guess I hate seeing the changes even though I understand the town couldn't stay the same after the factory closed." Her phone buzzed a timer warning. She tapped it off and stood. "I've got to get to the restaurant for the lunch crowd, but I want to check out some of these people afterwards. Marita is closing up today."

"Three o'clock?" He had stood too. He reached past her to remove her jacket from its hook, but he didn't just hand it to her.

He held it out for her to slip on. First one arm. Then the other. Then she turned, and he tugged the jacket's lapels together. For just a moment they stood like that. Her looking up. Him looking down. And then he smiled.

Oh, that smile. As if he knew something she didn't. The smile that had inspired her to draw countless tiny red hearts on her tenth-grade notebooks.

"I'll come by at three, okay?"

"Do you have time?"

"For you and Gran?" He held the door open for her as they moved outdoors. The weather had calmed overnight, and a pristine October day awaited them. "Always."

He waited as she got into her car, and he didn't even climb into his SUV until she'd backed out of the driveway. She headed up Merlin and down Bellwood. She'd learned to avoid Broadway this time of year. Parking in Sleepy Hollow was tough under everyday conditions. The much-needed fall tourists clogged parking lots and streets every September and October now that the town had embraced its Washington Irving roots. A large crowd had gathered at the Sleepy Hollow Cemetery's southern gate, excitedly waiting for a guided tour of the historic burial grounds. The cozy neighborhood streets on the west side of Broadway were dotted with dog walkers. Some were heading for the nearby park and others were enjoying the tree-lined streets.

This would be a good place to have a dog. And a great place to call home again, she admitted to herself. But at what cost? Would staying here negate all the years of effort she'd put into education and career-building in New York City? Most small towns didn't have a big need for investment bankers, although she could work remotely from anywhere these days. So that opened a wealth of possibilities.

Unless she decided to be a soup-maker instead.

She parked in the church parking lot on Beekman. The church had invited Gran to use their lot for some off-street parking when it wasn't conducting services. She locked the car and was cutting through the shaded path to Cortlandt Street when a man stepped out in front of her.

Her heart spiked an adrenaline rush. Her pulse jumped.

He stood there, blocking the path, saying nothing. Not big. But not small either.

The church behind her was empty. Beekman Street was busy as always, but trees and tall shrubs blocked the line of sight between Beekman and Cortlandt through the church lot. The big empty school on her right would be no help.

She swallowed hard and started to move back.

He came forward.

He had a gray stocking hat on. It covered his head, a little silly in light of the pleasant day, and he wore a thin blue medical mask. She couldn't see his face or even his hairline.

Dark eyes.

That's all she could see in the dappled shadows of the overgrown vegetation separating the church's land from its neighbors'.

She backed up.

He moved forward.

She fingered the cell phone in her right pocket and tugged her purse closer. If she turned to run, a quick grab from behind would stop her, but his menacing approach made running seem like the best option.

She started to turn.

He reached out.

At that very moment, Sister Rosalina Gonzalez called her name from the church parking lot. "Teresa! It is so good to see you, my young friend! Welcome home! *¿Cómo está tu abuela? ¿Todavía está en el hospital?*"

Chapter Three

Sister Rosalina had taught Spanish to junior high kids by leapfrogging her way between the languages both in and out of the classroom.

The man took off as soon as she spoke. He darted down the path and disappeared onto Cortlandt.

Tess took a breath—a deep one—to calm her pulse, then put her hand on the nun's arm. "Sister, did you recognize that man? The one who just ran toward Cortlandt Street?"

Sister Rosalina shook her head. "I didn't, dear. I'm sorry. I saw you get out of your car and hurried over to catch you. All I saw was a flash of blue as I came around the corner. And the gray hat," she added. "That seemed odd on a day when it's too warm for a hat, wouldn't you say? You look pale, Teresa. Like you've seen a ghost. Did he hurt you? Scare you?"

Tess held her breath just long enough to calm her nerves, a trick her father had taught her years before. "Let's say his sudden appearance was unsettling. There we were, face-to-face on the path, and he wouldn't move out of the way."

"I've told the council we need to get rid of these overgrown bushes," Sister Rosalina replied. "They started out as ornamentals, but now they've taken over the path. And the height of that old maple keeps this in shadow at night, even with the dusk-to-dawn lights on. It's a liability. I'll speak to them again. They're meeting this week."

"Sounds like a good idea to me," agreed Tess.

Sister Rosalina tapped something into her phone. When Tess sent her a questioning look, she gave a rueful laugh. "I'm texting it to myself so I don't forget. Sign of age, eh?"

"It's a sign of a woman who is devoted to helping her community," Tess said. The normalcy of the exchange calmed her nerves.

The man was gone. The retired teacher was beside her, and when Sister Rosalina motioned toward Cortlandt Street, Tess wasn't about to refuse the company. "You must be getting things ready for the big clothing and food drive," she said as they fell into step between the church buildings.

Sister Rosalina nodded as they navigated through the old schoolyard that abutted Gran's tiny parking area behind the building. "We used to do these things in November, but as the town recovered, we moved the fundraiser back to October. We fill the old school hall to the rafters, Tess. It's amazing. Tourists donate too, and that's an added blessing. Sometimes they buy food or new clothing to donate, but a lot of them just leave cash. Or checks. No one foresaw that as we were developing a tourism base. A lot of our small businesses make their profit margin in these eight weeks. They might break even the rest of the year, but the fall influx is huge. Our school hall is the main collection site in the village, but there are others up the hill."

Rising above the riverside towns were historic and beautiful hillside communities that joined in the charitable efforts.

"We also make a point to do some old-fashioned gleaning," Sister Rosalina added as they neared Gran's restaurant. "We keep a cache of food on hand right here. Some folks are too proud to sign up for the food cupboard or they fall between the cracks of eligibility. A few of us decided we could do something about that. And so we do."

"I've been told that between you and Gran there's little chance of anyone going hungry midwinter."

Rosalina stayed matter of fact. "Winters come and go. And friends help friends. Your grandma always said that losing your grandpa was hard, but he left her a paid-off house and business. Between the soup shop and the rent from the upstairs apartment, she's got enough money to get by. And what more does a body need than that? Working with your grandmother to help feed folks in the winter isn't a chore. It's an absolute privilege."

"That's Gran all right," Tess agreed. "Want to come in the back door with me?" she asked as they approached the narrow strip of asphalt behind the soup shop.

"I'm stopping over at the little Spanish bakery, then coming over for my soup and rolls. Sophia and I always split a quart of soup and bread every Monday."

Sophia was Sister Rosalina's older sister.

"It's our way of celebrating another beautiful weekend under our belts. I'll be back in just a few minutes, okay?"

"Okay. See you soon."

The little restaurant was packed.

Marita filled orders while Tess got busy baking.

Gran didn't do fancy, and she didn't vary the menu much. White bread, white rolls, chewy and fresh, but each time a new customer requested rye or wheat or artisan, Tess cringed. They could do that easily enough.

On the other hand, Gran had been running a successful business for decades, so Tess wasn't about to tell her what to do.

Marita popped back into the kitchen ten minutes later. "Sister Rosalina said some man bothered you. Who was it? Where was it?"

Tess brushed it off. "It wasn't a big deal, but I was glad she came along at the right time. The guy made me nervous."

"Was he waiting for you? Ambushing you?"

Tess shook her head quickly. Maybe too quickly. "I don't think so. He just kind of appeared out of nowhere."

"Which is, I believe, the definition of the word *ambush*. Tess, every now and then we get odd folks hanging around between the buildings."

"With the police department less than two blocks away?" asked Tess, surprised. The updated police and fire stations were nearby, on Beekman.

"No one can see between the big buildings," Marita told her. "It's just quiet enough and sheltered enough to let things happen out of sight. There've been a couple of arrests there over the past few years, and there's probably been stuff the cops haven't seen. You know that drug sales are a problem, even in small towns. As long as there are buyers, we'll have sellers."

A shiver chased down Tess's spine. "Is Gran aware of this?"

"No one would hurt Gran. Ever," declared Marita. "She does too much good for the town." She headed back toward the busy storefront. "But I'd like to know what this fellow looked like."

"He wore a gray stocking hat and a face mask. You know, the kind you wear when you're worried about passing germs."

Marita had been about to go through the door. Instead, she stopped and turned, one hand on the swinging door. "Why would anyone do that? Why would anyone target you?"

The conman?

Had he discovered that she was helping Gran track down the money? Was the encounter like Marita said? A possible ambush? Or a fear tactic?

It took effort to keep her voice mild. "No reason I can think of. Probably just a chance meeting on a skinny path."

It wasn't. She knew that, and she was pretty sure Sister Rosalina had figured it out too. Not much got by the former junior high teacher. But it came to nothing, and only made her more determined to figure out what happened to the money Gran had given and collected. When Riley showed up at five after three, she tossed her apron into the wash basket and carried it to the back door.

He took the basket from her as soon as she stepped out.

Then he tucked it into the rear of his SUV, rounded the car, and opened the door for her. "Where to?"

"Let's go see Susan Mary."

He winked. "The cat hater."

"Hey, I'm a dog person myself, but cats have their place. Downtown might be overrun with mice if Old Tom and Tillie weren't vigilant in their hunting excursions." Old Tom and Tillie had been feral cats several years ago. Gran and some others had taken to feeding them in the old wooden shed near the shared business dumpster, and the cats returned the favor by minimizing rodent concerns, one tasty critter at a time.

"Address?"

She gave him the address she'd found on the internet. Six minutes later they were parking along Susan Mary's curb.

Riley turned off the car and Tess reached for the door handle. "Let's go."

Riley didn't hesitate.

He liked helping her. And not just because of Gran. He'd realized that this morning because when she left to go to the restaurant, he hadn't wanted to let her go. That almost instant emotion created a new dynamic to his current puzzle. He got out of the car and spotted a woman in the yard and whistled softly. "That's Susan Mary?"

Tess followed his gaze through the trimmed shrubs. A young woman was plugging gorgeous chrysanthemums into a border garden. "I thought she'd be older. Like Gran."

"Clearly, we were both mistaken. Let's go."

The young woman kept working, oblivious to their presence until they shut their car doors.

That drew her attention.

She stood, peeled off her gardening gloves, and came their way. "Can I help you?"

Her tone belied the offer. She folded her arms, braced her legs, and locked eyes with Riley.

But Tess spoke first. "I'm Tess McIntosh. June McIntosh is my grandmother."

The woman squinted slightly, the only indication that the name meant anything.

"Gran runs the Sleepy Hollow Soup Shop on Cortlandt Street."

Susan Mary's expression didn't change. "I know who she is. I'm sure half the town does. A nice little old lady who passes time making soup and trying to fix this, that, and the other thing."

"She is known for her big heart," agreed Riley.

"Except it takes a lot more than big hearts to fix things that need fixing," stated Susan Mary. "But that's none of my business. Is there a reason for this visit? Because I'm busy. As you can see."

"Gorgeous mums." Tess admired the just-blooming flowers from her spot on the driveway. "Gran loves mums too. She says their longevity makes a garden come to life when nature says it's time to go to sleep."

"So we agree on something."

"But not on cats. Or dogs. Or stray animals," noted Riley.

She rolled her eyes. "I'm practical. I'm practical about most everything, and I don't get it when people get all fired up over saving every animal on the planet. There are plenty of humans needing help, and that's a fact. But humans have fallen out of favor, it seems."

"You told her that she should put her efforts into helping homeless people, not pets. And when one of her neighbors talked about contributing money for shelter animals, you said that money would be much better spent on helping people."

Susan Mary frowned. "I went further than that. I said I couldn't believe how much people would give for stray cats and dogs while the homeless are sleeping under bridges, and that if I had that cash, I'd be helping the ones living in tents midwinter. And I meant it."

"Did you mean it enough to create a fake foundation to get money from all those pet lovers and then use that money to help your cause?" asked Riley. He didn't have to wait long for her reaction.

"A fake—what?" Susan Mary looked astounded and insulted. "Are you accusing me of misrepresenting something? Or misappropriation of funds? I'm an accountant, and I promise you if I wanted to do it, I could. I have the skills. But why would anyone do that?"

"To teach a bunch of pet-loving old fogies a lesson?"

She'd used those very words in one of her comments, and when Riley repeated them, she drew a sharp breath.

"They got conned."

She looked from Riley to Tess and made a face. "This is exactly what I mean. You get a bunch of bleeding hearts on social media and anyone—and I mean *anyone*—can come up with a plan to scam you. What starts out as a simple conversation about a poor little puppy becomes a way to steal from a lot of people who probably can't afford it."

When Riley raised a brow, she skewered him with a dark look. "The mix of retirees and social media provides the perfect recipe for bilking. That's all I'm saying. Why would I tell you this if I'd done it?"

"Because the best defense is a good offense?" suggested Tess.

Susan Mary slapped her gloves against her hand. "Conversation over. I'm sorry that bunch of do-gooders got scammed, but they set themselves up for it by putting a target on their backs. All I can say is, they're fortunate to know a couple of people young enough to clean up the mess they made. Now, goodbye."

She turned and strode to the house.

Once they got back into the car, Riley faced Tess. "She made a great point."

"She's snarky and thinks seniors are gullible."

He nodded. "Yes, but she's likely innocent. She also gave us another slant on the investigation."

Tess frowned. "What kind of slant?"

"We only checked the comments to posts on Gran's Facebook page. We need to check the other donors' Facebook pages also. If this is, as it's starting to look like, a local con or grudge, then the thief is likely someone who followed their posts and conversations about his 'charity.'" He made quote marks with his fingers. "So let's check that all out. And Mom invited you for supper tonight. After you visit Gran. Sound good?"

He wanted it to sound good, and when she hesitated, he thought of fourteen reasons to convince her, but then she turned his way. And smiled. "It sounds great, actually."

Her reply eased his heart, but made it beat harder, an odd dynamic. She'd said yes.

That was enough. For now.

He drove north to the hospital, and after they'd parked and walked inside, Tess headed toward the elevator to go see Gran. He paused in the spacious lobby.

She got about six feet before she turned. "Aren't you coming?"

"I don't want to intrude," he began, but then she came back to him, grabbed hold of his arm, and tugged him forward. "O'Toole, we have a tough old gal who's a little under the weather, a restaurant to run, a couple of cats to care for, supper waiting, and a crime to solve. No time to worry about intruding now."

He'd be a fool to resist, and Riley O'Toole was nobody's fool.

They went up to the cardiac unit and found Gran chomping at the bit to go home. The charge nurse followed them into the room. "She's looking better, isn't she?"

Gran glowered. "Nothing I'm doing here that I can't do at home, Janet Degler, and you know it."

"Except you need to accept your fate until tomorrow morning," Janet shot back. "Your current mission is to veg with bad TV, read a book, or sleep. Doctor Hollister says we'll spring you first thing tomorrow. Can you pick her up then, Tess?"

"If she's nice." Tess scolded her grandmother with a dour look, then leaned down and kissed her cheek. "How're you doing, Gran? Really?"

Gran rolled her eyes, a move Riley remembered from decades before, then she sighed. A big, overdone, well-practiced sigh. "I'm better. And better yet by seeing you two. How are things at the restaurant? I can't wait to get back there. It's October, for heaven's sake, all those tourists—"

Janet cleared her throat. "No work yet. You need to get your meds regulated and we need to make sure your heart is stable. Just a reminder, Gran." She leaned in to underscore her point. "Hearts are essential to life." She deadpanned a frown aimed at Gran before she turned to leave the room. "See you later."

Gran faced them once Janet had rounded the corner. "Give me what you've got, and don't hold back. I'm doing fine, they've got things under control, and we need to catch this creep!"

Riley had forgotten how much he appreciated the small-town personalities that peppered Sleepy Hollow. "We've started to dig. We can't report any positive results yet, but we've narrowed the scope of our search, and that's the first step toward solving the mystery."

"And you?" Gran turned her attention to Tess.

She pointed to Riley. "What he said. Give us time, Gran. Okay?"

Gran scowled, then righted her expression. "Of course. And Doc Hollister told me not to get riled over things. He gave me a long lecture this morning, about how I'm not an anxious person so why start being overwrought now? I guess that makes sense," she went on. "He's right, I don't fret. I'm a doer. But the thought of someone taking that money for their own nefarious means shook me up. And that's the truth of it."

"First, great word." Riley made sure to look really impressed, and Gran smiled. "Second, the shop is doing great, Tess is amazing, Marita has stepped right up to work extra hours, and we have a couple of leads. I promise you, we're not putting the hunt on the back burner, but we're also taking care of business."

"It is. Stealing makes me angry, and not being able to run things is about the most frustrating thing ever. I've caught the flu twice in the last fifteen years. Other than that, I've never missed a day at the soup shop." She paused. Glanced down. Then back up at them, and her expression turned glum. "This whole kerfuffle made me realize that time is marching on."

"Oh, good grief," said Tess. "Haven't you heard? Seventy is the new fifty, and it looks good on you. You know why you should be counting your blessings?"

Gran's wince said she was probably about to find out.

"Because we have great health care, the likes of which you're getting now, and you have wonderful people stepping up to the plate. And I picked now to come home, Gran. To be on hand. It's like—"

"A God-gift," said Gran. Then she yawned. "Things like this don't happen by accident, Tessie."

"I haven't heard you called Tessie in a long, long time." Riley bumped shoulders with her. "It's cute."

"For a nine-year-old. Or"—Tess leaned down and swept butterfly kisses to Gran's cheek—"from the Gran you love so much. You rest. We're having supper with Riley's mom and then we'll be back on the job. Both jobs. Love you, Gran."

"I love you too. You'll be here in the morning, first thing? To bust me out?"

"Absolutely. Once the bread racks are filled. Then I'm dropping you at home so I can make soup with Marita. I'll bring you a warm loaf of bread when I come pick you up, okay?"

"Nothing better. Thank you, Tess. And you too, Riley."

"My pleasure, Gran." They turned to go, but then Tess drew back.

"Gran, have you ever considered adding rye or wheat to the bread list? That chewy honey wheat is wildly popular at restaurants now."

"Why mess with success?" asked Gran. She yawned again.

Tess almost argued with her, then thought better of it. "You're right. Good night, Gran."

"G'night."

He waited until they got to the elevator to question her. "You want to add things to the menu, Tessie? Pretty radical of you."

She smacked his arm. "There's nothing wrong with trying things out. Spreading our wings. But I don't want to rile Gran up with new ideas. I can talk to her about it when things calm down."

"Which will be?" The elevator opened. They stepped in and even the antiseptic scents of hospital cleansers didn't overpower how wonderful Tess smelled. A bit of home-baked bread, fruity shampoo and just—her.

"After we find the crook, make hundreds community of gallons of soup, thousands of loaves of bread, and help with the Thanksgiving dinners. January?" She tipped her gaze up to his. "Maybe?"

He was supposed to go back to Rochester then. Back to the townhouse between the quarreling neighbors, back to his office, back to a daily routine that didn't allow time for solving internet scams on old people when corporations were paying hundreds of thousands for Centurion Industries to keep their web presence safe.

But he'd figure that out later. "Then January it is. Let's get your car and head to Mom's. Okay? It's not quiet at the house," he warned. "But it's the best thing that could have happened for her right now."

Chapter Four

Kathy O'Toole made a stew that rivaled Gran's, and Tess didn't hesitate to say so. "I've never had better. And with the nights cooling off, this hits the spot."

"Comfort food," Kathy replied. She had wavy dark brown hair that she kept off her face with one of those stretchy headbands. It was an old-fashioned look that suited her. "Food like this is really satisfying when the days grow short. People don't go out as much once the daylight fades early. Or maybe it's that everyone orders in for delivery. It's different with the Sleepy Hollow Soup Shop," she went on as Carrie loaded the dishwasher. Her two kids had dashed upstairs with Riley—*noisily*—to get pajamas on. "Folks come in, grab their quarts or half-gallons, and head out, all set. But I've noticed that the waterfront places are quieter earlier now. Of course, my schedule's changed up too."

Carrie shot her mother a look Kathy didn't see. Concern and sympathy deepened her features. "People are creatures of habit. They got used to ordering in and realized how easy that was. You know what they say. Anything you do for thirty days becomes a habit."

"There's a lot of truth in that," agreed Tess. "Carrie, Riley said that you're the assistant principal of your school now."

"I got the appointment when Dad was sick." Carrie closed the dishwasher and hit the power button. "I almost didn't take it because

I was afraid time was growing short, but he gave me a stern talking-to."

Kathy sighed softly. "He was good at that, but he was also an absolute marshmallow."

"He was. Riley definitely gets his tough side from you, Mom," Carrie teased. "Dad was the iconic salesman," she went on, directing her attention back to Tess. "He listened to people. He never tried to change their minds unless he realized that what they wanted didn't match what they could afford, and he sized that up quickly. He always said if he sold them more boat than they needed he'd never be able to erase that sour feeling they'd have. And sour feelings are the downfall of good business."

"Gran's the same way on a lesser scale," said Tess. "She meets people's needs, and that's what drives her success."

"Both good people." Kathy reached down to pet the tail-wagging corgi at her feet. It was a seriously cute dog, and Tess wasn't generally a fan of small dogs. "The profit margins might be different, but I expect Gran wrestles with the same financial issues Boyd did."

"Property taxes make sure of that," declared Carrie. "I love our town, but the proximity to the city has driven taxes through the roof."

Tess hadn't given much thought to that since coming home. "I didn't realize," she told them. "I know being self-employed puts Gran in a tough tax bracket, but I've never had to pay property taxes. They're high?"

Kathy nodded. "Very. And Gran owns her house plus the property on Cortlandt Street, so she gets hit twice."

That had to be why Gran referred to the upstairs rental on Cortlandt Street as the restaurant's saving grace. "I had no idea."

Riley came down the steps, hooked a thumb to the stairs, and addressed Carrie. "Your turn. Bathroom, teeth, pajamas, and two stories are complete. They're ready to be tucked in."

"Thank you, Riley." She fist-bumped his arm as she went by him. "Best little brother ever."

Kathy said, "Hodgins needs a look outside about now, I expect."

"We can take him, Mom." Riley took his and Tess's jackets out of the stairway closet. "You up for a little walk, Tess? With two cool guys? Me and the pooch?"

He made her laugh. He made her think. And he still made her dream. But he'd be leaving soon, and she'd be staying. "I've been longing for some fresh air all day. I expect Hodgins and I could both use a nice stroll by the river."

The corgi perked up when she said his name. He trotted her way on those short stocky legs and peered up at her with trusting brown eyes. The kind of eyes that won the heart straight off.

Riley snapped a lead to the dog's collar. "Come on, Hodge. Let's take a look around Horan's Landing."

Riley dropped the leash, then turned to help Tess with her jacket. She could get used to this. Real used to it.

Her heart sped up.

She tamped it down.

Letting fifteen-year-old emotions rule any part of the current-day situation was silly. But as they strolled to the waterfront park and the beautiful new memorial garden overlooking the mighty river, it felt right. Her. Him. The funny little dog and the beautiful setting. "This is amazing." She indicated the pristine expanse of the new Edge-on-Hudson development, a long-term project that provided a much-needed facelift on the abandoned old manufacturing site. "And so beautifully done."

Trimmed-out four-story townhouses stood sentinel along the river's edge. The developers had made room for ground-level businesses facing the village. Above that row, the townhomes rose in splendor, with views of the majestic Hudson on one side, the Manhattan skyline on the other, and the rising hills stretching to their east. And in between, the hometown feel of Sleepy Hollow drew people in. She indicated the array of new buildings that had replaced the decaying nineteenth-century automotive factory site. "The promenade out to the lighthouse is wonderful. And even though I made crazy good money in Lower Manhattan, I can't imagine being able to afford a place like this. Although they're gorgeous."

"I'm staying in that one." Riley jutted his chin toward a south-facing group of townhomes, and when she looked surprised, he shrugged. "One of the Centurion investors owns it. He's in Europe for a year. He offered the keys when he heard about my dad and Carrie's remodeling. He figured I'd get more work done without Bailey and Brandon underfoot."

"Wow."

"Wanna see it?"

"Yes!" She laughed. "How often do I get to tour million-dollar homes, Riley? Is it okay to bring Hodge in?"

"A lot of the owners have dogs. And some of them have dog-walkers, but yes. Hodge comes to visit on a regular basis. Come on. Let me show you how the other half lives."

"I'd say it's more like the top one percent," she said, then sighed when he opened the door. "It's pretty, Riley."

"It's amazing," he agreed as he swung the door shut. "But I realized something when I moved in."

"And that is?"

He motioned her up the stairway to her left, and when they got to the second floor, he waved a hand. "I want more."

"More than a million-dollar place?" She whistled. "That's a little greedy, don't you think, Mr. O'Toole?"

He laughed. "Not bigger or better. I want more than the classic narrow profile of townhouses. I want a house," he said simply. "With rooms side by side. With noise and maybe neighbors throwing block parties and having barbecues. That was the norm when we were growing up. Remember?"

"I remember all right. You and Bridget were the talk of the town back then, the toast of the in-crowd."

"I didn't know high schools had in-crowds," he argued as they continued up the next flight of stairs. He led the way to the balcony.

"Everyone knows high schools have in-crowds, and you and my sister were the innest of all. But nice try."

He'd just opened the door leading to the small but open balcony.

He paused.

Turned.

And then he grinned. "Were you jealous, Tess?"

She made a face of denial, then shrugged. "Nothing wrong with wanting to be cool. In tenth grade, anyway."

"I suppose not." He'd picked up Hodge so the little fellow wouldn't try to explore between the railings, although Hodge was pudgy enough that it might not be an issue. "I mean of me? And your sister?" One look at her face and he knew, and he could have teased her, he could have made light of a young girl's emotions and longings.

He didn't.

He had Hodgins in one strong arm.

He brought the other hand up to her cheek and palmed her face. "I'm sorry, Tess. I never knew."

"Well, you weren't supposed to know, because you'd fallen in love with my sister. End of story."

"Not love."

She skewered him with a look.

"Not real love, Tess. High school stuff. She moved on, I moved on, you moved on. And now we're adults. It's different. We're different. But if that blush is any indication, Tess McIntosh, I think maybe we're not so different after all. Hmm?"

She would have stepped away, but there was no room to do that, so they stood there, face-to-face, the cool breeze wafting off the river as it had done for thousands of years. "Tess." He dropped his gaze to her mouth in question, a question she didn't dare answer.

She turned slightly, then paused and pointed. "Can you imagine the view from up there?"

The quick change of subject didn't fool him, but he didn't pressure her. He nodded as he looked up. "Hobb's Hill. It's got a whole line of upscale shops and eateries that overlook the river. Manhattan prices. Beautiful views. Maybe we could go there for dinner sometime? Without Hodge."

She reached out to pet the dog, and when she did, her hand touched Riley's. It felt like she knew it would. Perfect. She drew a breath and smiled. "I'd love to have dinner with you, Riley O'Toole. That would be delightful. But it doesn't have to be expensive."

He smiled down.

She smiled up. "My gran is a soup-maker, remember? I come from simple roots. Simple makes me happy."

"I can do simple, Tess. Let's get Gran on her feet, and you and I can go exploring."

"Exploring the town we've known all our lives?"

She moved back inside. He followed and closed the balcony door behind them. "Maybe exploring what this is all about?"

He indicated the space between them with a questioning expression.

She refused to take the bait. "It's about a quick walk back to your mom's because I'll be making soup and proofing bread in six-and-a-half hours. And..." She yawned. "The thought of staying up late doesn't even occur to me these days."

"Good point."

She led the way downstairs and out the front door. Riley handed her the leash. She waited while he locked the door, and when he came her way, she offered the leash back to him.

He didn't take it.

He took her other hand instead.

Instant warmth. Instant connection, exactly how she'd always known it would be.

He winked at her when she paused. "You don't mind walking him, do you?"

"You know I don't."

"Well, then." He gave her hand a light squeeze. "Let's head back so you can get home. And tomorrow we'll meet with Gran to find out anything and everything we don't know."

"We can't upset her."

He laughed. "Being out of the loop is probably far worse than talking things through, if I know Gran."

He was right. He was right about Gran, about holding hands, and about moving forward. She put her worries and questions on hold and let the lovely evening and the wonderful company take precedence. They had a crime to solve. Sure, they could go to the local police, but as a financial investor she understood the layers of work it took to examine internet crime. So did Riley. The local police were inundated with the October influx of people and vehicles. For the next few weeks, the matter of a handful of senior citizens willingly giving their money to a scammer would never make top priority.

It couldn't.

But between her and Riley?

It absolutely could.

Chapter Five

Gran was home and resting comfortably.

The Tuesday lunch rush was over, but they had plenty of soup for the late-afternoon takeout crowd, and she'd arranged tomorrow's recipes with Marita and Sonya, Marita's fifteen-year-old daughter.

Rolls were made, bread was baked, bagged, and tagged, and Tess took a quick trip up to Gran's house once things calmed down. She'd meet Riley at Gran's, have a quick discussion on the missing funds, then get back to work.

Wrong.

Cars lined both sides of Gran's street. That was problematic on the narrow streets of Sleepy Hollow even in the off-season, so it was bound to get people upset to have the street blocked to two-way traffic in October.

Tess wasn't sure what to expect, but the focused orderliness of the people inside was a surprise.

Two men and a woman were in a deep discussion in the front room, a half-dozen others were staked out in the kitchen, and four more were gathered around Gran in the dining area. Gran was jotting something down. She spotted Tess and waved her over. "Look who's here!" she announced to anyone listening. "One of my highly-skilled internet-savvy detectives has arrived and is on the case! We'll get to the bottom of these hijinks yet."

Tess did her best to put on a confident expression before she leaned down and whispered in Gran's ear. "Aren't you supposed to be resting? And avoiding stress?"

"Over twenty-thousand missing simoleons *is* a stress," Gran whispered back. "Good folk gathering to track it down is a blessing," she finished.

"You told them?" She kept her voice soft.

"Didn't have to," Gran replied. "A couple of the donors went to the website to see if there were new animals in trouble and discovered it was gone."

"And when we heard that June's ticker went wonky, we got together," said a woman. "I'm M.E. Martin, most folks call me Em and forget that it's not Emily, which is a total bother, but with so many years behind me and not near as many in front, I just shrug it off. No sense gettin' upset over things we can't change when the Good Lord gives us plenty we can. Like those poor neglected creatures. We're all in this together, and not one of us wanted June to take this on her shoulders, so we gathered round to show her."

Tess appreciated the combined efforts, but she had to keep Gran's physical health front and center. "Aren't you tired, Gran?"

"Tired?" Gran shot her a look of surprise. "I'm the opposite of tired. I'm rarin' to go, and if I don't have the clearance to hoof it around town, these folks do." She made a quick round of introductions. Tess knew six people. The rest were complete strangers to her. But not to Gran.

"My vote goes to your crotchety neighbor down there by the soup shop, June." Marge Abernathy had been their friend for decades. She crossed the room, set down a plate of cookies, and took a seat with Gran. Tess followed suit. "I've never seen a body get that upset over badly parked cars, and he went ballistic last spring when the town agreed to host that 5K race to kick off the fall tourist season."

"Derrick," said Gran.

Tess typed his name into her phone notes. "What's his last name?"

"Van Orden," Marge told her. "He's made it his mission to go to every single meeting on every little thing because he claims we don't have the right infrastructure to handle all we want to do and we should fix that first, then bring people in. Trouble is, if we wait until we have the money to fix things up, it won't happen, because there's no money in the till. When it comes to math, Derrick's not the sharpest tool in the shed. He's a grudge holder, and he likes to even up the score. His words," she added. "Not mine. He tops my list."

"He lives on Cortlandt Street?"

Gran shook her head. "Around the corner. On Depeyster. Near the old school entrance. And folks do pull up around the corner and double park. I'm sure it's a nuisance, but it's only during lunch and dinner. And weekends. And pretty much all fall."

Tess grimaced. "He might have a legitimate beef if that's the case. Has anyone offered him some constructive solutions? Is he the only one complaining?"

"He's the primary one," interjected a woman who joined them at the table. "He's a typical Van Orden. They get put out easy, always did according to my grandmother, God rest her soul. He's got some spite added to the mix because his sister wanted to work at the soup shop and Gran didn't hire her."

"So he's really angry," said Tess.

"It was nearly twenty years back." Gran sounded understandably doubtful.

"But the parking problem is current," the new woman reasoned. "I'm Dottie Jackson, by the way," she said to Tess, "from the clerk's office, and Derrick's one of those folks that… Well, let's just say some people cross the street when they see him coming. He's gotten dour in his later years. He's even wearing a mask everywhere he goes to drive home the point that all these strangers are bringing new germs into the area."

A mask?

Was Derrick Van Orden the scary guy lurking between the Sleepy Hollow Soup Shop and St. Teresa's church? She would definitely check him out.

Another woman and two men joined them from the kitchen. The woman carried sliced apples of all colors colorfully arranged around a dish of caramel.

One of the men had a stack of napkins, and the second brought a pitcher and set it in the center of the table.

"Iced tea," he announced in a voice that hinted culture.

"Carl and Philip, thank you." Gran jotted something else down in her notebook. "Do either of you have ideas?"

The cultured man shook his head. "I don't, I'm sorry to say. There's no proximity from my place to your soup kitchen—"

"Soup *shop*," said Dottie, stressing the second word. "The Sleepy Hollow Soup *Shop*. June helps out her share of people, but it's not a soup kitchen. It's a woman-run business that sets a good example for everyone in this town, and it burns me every time you call it a soup kitchen, Philip."

The man raised his hands, palms out, and looked bored. "It's soup, isn't it, Dorothy? But if it offends you, then of course." He offered a shrug that said offending her wasn't something he cared about one way or the other. "I'll correct my verbiage. I simply meant I'm not close enough to offer an opinion on this man because I'm up the hill. Please accept my apology."

"Accepted." Dottie said the word primly before she retreated to meet up with the crew in the front room.

"I'll check Derrick out," Tess promised. "And we're—"

She was interrupted by Riley coming in the front door. "We're following every lead," she said as he came to her side. "Aren't we, Riley?"

"There aren't too many yet, so we appreciate everything you all are doing. I'm sure that will help move things along."

When everyone stopped talking to hang on his every word, Tess realized he had that touch. That undefinable charisma that made people pay attention. Of course, he was crazy good looking and smart and smooth. The same combination of factors that tugged her heart all those years before.

Then he suggested that everyone gather in the dining room. "I'm going to ask you all to do me a favor. A big favor," he added, and when he flashed that amazing smile, Tess was pretty sure several aging hearts fluttered. "In all my years of tracking down online crime, one thing I've discovered is that these people are smart. Really smart. I'm concerned that if too many of us are nosing around, we might scare him or her off. We think they're local, but they might not be," he reminded them. "If you could give me your leads, Tess and I will follow up on them. We can form an online group and I'll keep you informed of everything we find. That way we're all in the know, but the thief is left blind. If that meets with your approval." He swept the group a look, and everyone nodded. "All I need is an email list, and we'll get this taken care of."

"I've got paper right here," declared Gran, and in five minutes, they had everyone's name, address, phone number, and email written down.

Gran's clock chimed three times.

Tess grabbed her purse and slung it over her shoulder. "Gotta head back. Nice meeting you all, and between me and Riley, we're going to do everything we can to find your money. I know how bad Gran feels about this whole thing because she tries to do the right thing for so many. We'll see you soon."

She threaded her way through the people.

Riley followed and when they got to the street, he had to go one way and she had to go the other.

She hated that.

When she looked up to say goodbye, his expression said he hated it too. And then it didn't happen, because Riley didn't head to his car.

He walked to hers. He opened the door for her, saw that she was settled in, and closed it snugly.

She opened the window and he leaned down. "See you back here at six, okay?"

"Lovely."

He grinned, reached in, and stroked one finger against her cheek. When she arched a brow in question, his smile deepened. "Just wanted to see if it was as soft as I thought."

"And the result?" She asked it as if it were a technical question, not a delightful flirtation.

"Softer."

She sighed inside. "Riley."

He grinned and winked. "See you at six."

She drove back to the soup shop, and she wasn't thinking about the missing money. She was thinking of how silly it was to let her heart get tangled up again when she knew there was no future for them.

The church lot wasn't being used today, but her face-to-face with the masked man made her hesitate. She drove down the road. There was no curbside parking, and the spots behind the shop were full, which meant she had to use the church lot after all.

She pulled in and parked. Then she drew a deep breath and climbed out.

What were the odds that the same man would be there today? Hopefully zero.

But just in case, she took the long way around Beekman. The beautiful fall day had people out in droves. If it was this busy on an October Tuesday, the coming weekend would be crazier than the last one.

She passed the group of patio tables lining the corner intersection and drew up short.

The man was there, on Cortlandt, coming her way, mask and all. He moved with purpose, and he aimed straight for her.

She didn't go on the defensive.

She mimicked his tactics like a well-planned offense. She strode his way, one firm footfall after another, and when he stopped, so did she. Then, arms folded, she faced him. "What is it you want, and why are you bothering my grandmother? And let me remind you, we're in a wide-open space, mister. So don't try anything. Got it?"

"I've got it all right," he shot back. Her strong stance didn't seem to intimidate him at all. "And you know what else I'm going to have? A court order to make that grandma of yours figure out the parking problem on her dime, because the town's about to start listening to me. And about time too. I've got a lawyer and I aim to make sure someone starts paying attention. Starting with this town and June McIntosh!"

Chapter Six

Riley hadn't intended to follow Tess to the soup shop, but when he saw that a fender bender had snarled traffic on Gordon, he had no choice but to head her way. Right before he turned off Gordon, he saw something that gave him pause. Then he headed down Beekman and took the turn onto Cortlandt.

And there was Tess, face-to-face with a masked man.

Riley didn't hesitate, nor did he look for one of the hard-to-find parking spots.

He double-parked, jumped out of the car, and raced to Tess's side. "What's going on here?"

She was fuming. Not scared. That was good, but the thought that this guy found it acceptable to challenge a young woman in the street spiked Riley's blood pressure.

"This doesn't concern you." The man half-growled the words.

"If it concerns Tess or Gran, it concerns me," Riley assured him. "And I don't take kindly to seeing my friends being intimidated. Who are you?"

"I'm Derrick Van Orden. And I don't care who you are, young man, it means nothing to me if you can't solve the fact that June McIntosh's customers don't care a whit about a person getting in or out of their driveway. Hard enough with everyone turning their places into rentals and having so many cars now. Then it gets much worse when it snows. It's ridiculous."

"I'm pretty sure neither my grandmother nor I can be blamed for snow," Tess answered him, and there was no mistaking the cool note in her voice. "Or people moving in and out. So you've gotten yourself a lawyer?"

"I've gotten the help I need because there's not a person that will listen to me without some legal expertise. After uselessly banging my head against a brick wall, I figured out it's not what you know, it's who."

"Lawyers are pricey. Especially lawyers anywhere near the city." Riley made the observation in an even tone.

"Son, everything around here's gotten pricey since we've gotten so full of ourselves. Used to be those with money kept to their places up the hill. Now they're everywhere, moving in here, there, and the other place. As if we don't have enough problem with clogging up roads and businesses with all this Headless Horseman nonsense. We used to be a small place for normal folks. Never mind." He huffed and charged past Tess, still angry. "Young folks like you don't know a thing about it. I'll see your grandmother in court. We'll see who's right and who's wrong then."

Head down, he walked away. He nearly plowed into a pair of women about to take an outdoor seat at the corner eatery, and he did bump into a man walking a dog. A familiar-looking, well-dressed man wearing a French beret. A funny little dog, with a smushed face, like a miniature bulldog.

Riley turned his attention to Tess once Derrick was out of sight. "Did he scare you?"

"Initially, yes, even though we're in the wide open here. But the more he talked, the more I realized the guy might have a legitimate beef. With so many businesses here on Cortlandt, the parking gets eaten up quickly."

"I thought that too. I know I'd be upset if I couldn't get out when I need to. Do you have five minutes?" He motioned to the cross-street. "Let's move my car and check out his place."

In two minutes, they pulled up in front of Derrick Van Orden's house, and Riley spotted the problem right off. "He's got no off-street parking. So if the street spots are filled—"

"He's got to find some place to park and walk back to his house. Which isn't the end of the world, but did you notice his limp?"

Riley nodded. "That might be exacerbating the problem. A lot of people think it's good for the town to move forward with the developers' ideas, but the ordinary citizen can get shafted. It's not easy to find an affordable house here now, owning or renting."

"Or one that doesn't need a flight of stairs to access," noted Tess. "I've noticed that the climbs around here are tough on a lot of people. The downside of having the town built on a hill."

Her phone pinged a text and she winced. "Oops. Marita. Gotta get in there and help."

Already cars were pulling off to the curb along Cortlandt. Once those spots were filled, people would park wherever they could to get their soup or bread or whatever goods they needed from the businesses lining the busy one-way street.

Riley pulled up by the back door to drop her off. "See you at Gran's in a bit. All right?"

"Yes. And Riley?"

He was about to back out of the parking area. He paused. "Yeah?"

She smiled. "Thanks for the rescue."

"I realize now you didn't need it, but I won't deny I was glad to do it, Tess."

Her smile deepened. "It was appreciated."

Her appreciation made him want to do more.

He hadn't had a chance to tell her what he'd seen on Gordon Avenue, but he had time to get to the town offices before everyone went home for the evening. He didn't leave there with answers, but he gathered some information that might lead to answers, and that might be a help for Derrick Van Orden's problem. He got in ninety minutes of work before it was time to head to Gran's, and when he turned onto her street, quiet reigned. Other than Tess's car, the driveway was empty. He parked and walked toward the door, but the fragrance of grilled meat tugged him to the backyard.

Gran waved a spatula in greeting. "Soup's good an' all, but a body needs a nice bit of meat now and again, don't you think, Riley?"

"I'm a meat-and-potatoes guy, so you've won my heart, Gran. Although I do like soup."

"Just not every day," she noted. She flipped the burgers with ease, then nodded to the house. "Tess is making macaroni salad. I had it all done. All she's got to do is mix it up good. I didn't want her to have to worry about cooking when she's been cooking off and on all day. It's nice enough to eat outside, but the kitchen gives us more privacy."

Riley held the plate as she took the burgers off the grill. "Sounds good."

A half hour later he leaned back in his chair. It was undeniably one of the best meals he'd ever had.

Burgers, cooked over a charcoal grill.

Mac salad, old-style. With tuna and mayo, the kind he loved and no one made anymore. He'd helped himself to probably more than he should have, then sighed when his plate was empty. "I haven't had mac salad like this since—"

He stopped abruptly before he finished the sentence, but Tess finished it for him.

"Since you were dating my sister?"

"No one makes mac salad like Gran." He figured if he said it with authority, Bridget might be left out of the conversation.

"I'm not sure why folks have to drive one thing out of style when they glom on to another, but that's the way of it," said Gran. "I like that new macaroni mix-up too, with the meats and the cheese and the dressings. You can throw most anything in there and it's good, but this old-style with mayo is a crowd-pleaser from way back. Like a good tuna sandwich and no need of bread. But that's not what we need to talk about."

"I've got something to share," said Riley. He stood to help clear the table. "When I left here earlier, I saw something odd. It was the Andreas woman."

"Susan Mary."

He nodded. "She was sneaking around Gordon Avenue where it comes into Katrina. Just before Broadway."

"Those spots fill up fast this time of year," said Tess. She rinsed the plates he handed her while Gran put the salad away. "Even though the signs say cars'll be towed if the people aren't using the businesses there, nobody wants to bite the tourist hand that feeds them, so it's more like first come, first serve in the fall. But I want to hear more about the sneaking part."

"She was furtive," he told them. "Slipping behind vehicles. Glancing around. Trying not to be seen."

"Doesn't make a lot of sense," said Gran. "She has no trouble spouting off about this and that on the internet. Why sneak around?"

"Unless she's guilty of something and didn't want to be seen?" Tess raised her hands when Gran looked doubtful. "Gran, I don't know why someone would engineer a group like All Creatures and then steal the money, but someone did. And if it turns out to be someone local—"

"And that brings me to another thing," Riley said. "Some of those pictures the person used *are* of local cats and dogs. Others were taken from random websites. Whoever did it replaced the captions but didn't know to replace the identifiers in the pictures, so I was able to trace them back to an earlier posting."

"You can tell all that from a photo?" asked Gran.

Riley put the plates into the dishwasher as he answered. "Sometimes. That's part of my job, Gran. Sometimes businesses hire me to design a web presence that can't be infiltrated, but other times, when it's too late for that, they hire me to figure out who's doing the infiltrating."

"So what does all that mean?" asked Gran. She motioned to the coffeepot. "I brewed fresh while we were eating. I know a lot of folks don't do after-supper coffee anymore, but I don't see harm in it and I'm old, so I'll do as I please. Who'd like to join me?"

"I'll pour," offered Tess. "You grab that cake thing someone brought—"

"Philip would cry to hear you call his marjolaine 'cake,'" said Gran. "His pastry chef supplies some of those fancy restaurants in Manhattan, and Philip says he's a stickler for authenticity. I don't even want to think what a pastry like this would cost. He assured me that even though this was about to be pulled from the case because it came in on Friday, it will still be one of the most delicious things on the planet."

Tess brought plates back to the table. Little ones. With small forks. "Gran always says the presentation enhances the experience."

"I don't think I've ever said any such thing, but I do like my desserts on dessert plates, that's a fact. And this…" She savored a first bite of the dessert. "Is melt-in-your-mouth amazing. So Riley, what's your take on Susan Mary?" she asked as they settled in with dessert. "Why would she be sneaking around? In broad daylight? That makes no sense."

"I don't know," he replied. "I made a list of businesses in the area." He handed them each a copy of the list he'd printed up. "Nothing stands out."

He was right. Susan Mary had picked a nondescript corner to sneak around, so why? And did it have anything to do with their visit the previous day? "She likes flowers," mused Tess. "Is there a garden store tucked along Katrina now?"

Gran shook her head. "Just a few shops and the animal hospital on the main road before you get to the big health clinic at the corner. Maybe she had a doctor's appointment?"

"I don't know why you'd skulk around to keep a doctor's appointment," said Riley. "But I'm too busy loving this cake to think clearly right now."

"It's crazy good," agreed Tess. "The health practice at that corner has gotten really big with solid online reviews. So that would make sense, except—" She frowned. "Why be furtive?"

"It wasn't natural," said Riley. He slid his phone her way. "I got two quick pics before she got behind the next vehicle."

Tess examined the picture. Then she shook her head and handed his phone to Gran. "I've got nothing," she admitted. "But then, my meeting with Derrick Van Orden put Susan Mary on the back burner."

"He came into the shop?" asked Gran. "He hardly ever does that. Most of the time he just glowers through the window when he passes by."

"He didn't come in. We had an unexpected meetup on the sidewalk. He knew who I was—"

"Why is that?" Riley inserted the question before she could go on. "Why would he know who you are if you've only been back here a few weeks?"

"Because her proud grandma has pictures of her and Bridget in the soup shop," admitted Gran. "I do boast on my grandbabies, I can't deny it."

"And we don't mind a bit," Tess told her. "Although it *is* my high school graduation picture, so we might want to update the brag book, Gran."

"And who'd have thought you'd get even prettier?" Riley paused eating the cake to meet her gaze. "I would have called it impossible."

Oh, her heart. Why did it have to grip so tight when her eyes met his? And why did the Good Lord plant him right here in front of her when she needed to stay and he needed to leave? "You're schmoozing me to get that last piece of Marjorie's Lane—"

"Marjolaine," scolded Gran, but she said it with a smile.

"But you needn't bother, because I think we should give it to Marita tomorrow morning. She'd love it. She goes to the Hispanic bakery near us a couple of times a week. She says their cakes are her guilty pleasure."

Riley disputed her words. "Wasn't after more cake." He flashed his smile. "Just citing facts, ma'am."

"Facts? Or flirting?" Tess aimed a stern look his way, but it did nothing to squelch his smile or the uptick in her pulse.

Gran got the conversation back on track. "Cake or no cake, Derrick worries me, but not on account of the missing money," she told them. "He's an unhappy man. Unhappy from the inside out. Has been for a while. I've reached out to him a number of times, but it goes nowhere. He's mad at me, mad at changes in the town, mad at life. I heard he lost his pension in some bankruptcy filing a year or so back."

Riley winced. "A lot of pensions went underwater with that filing," he said. "It's crushed a lot of people. Losing a pension can be a significant loss of income. And money is the likely motive for a scam like this."

"Which puts the spotlight on him," said Tess, but then she paused. "Although if you'd just bilked over twenty thousand dollars from someone, would you challenge them in the street? I'd have guessed the thief would go low profile. Not want to draw attention to himself. Or herself. When you passed Susan Mary this afternoon, did you see her go into any particular business?"

Riley shook his head. "No. I was waiting to make a left turn, so I only caught a couple of glimpses. When I got a clear spot to do a U-turn, I did. And lost sight of her."

"Then we keep her on the list." Tess typed a note into her phone and sat back, but she didn't miss Gran's look of concern. "What's wrong, Gran?"

"I feel foolish."

Tess started to protest, but Gran raised her hand, so Tess paused. "I've always prided myself on my good sense. I run a business, I'm past president of several volunteer organizations, and I raised two wonderful kids. I've been an active part of my grandchildren's lives, and no one's ever fooled me before. This time I let it happen."

"Gran—"

"No, let me finish." Gran seemed determined to get this off her chest, so Tess sat back again. "I let the website's pictures and posts draw me in, step by step. After a few weeks I watched for the 'All Creatures' postings to see what they'd done. Whoever did this drew us in by posting not just the sad things, but the happy times. Animals finding families. People being reunited with pets. Furbabies finding forever homes. I let myself get sucked in without really knowing anything about the group or the site or the person behind it. That's the foolish part," she insisted. "Not the donating. I like helping others, and I've got a soft spot for cats, but I let myself get played like a big fish on a ten-pound line, and that's the embarrassment. Money comes and goes. I'm not broke. But being fooled like that makes me want to hang my head."

"A good heart is never an embarrassment," said Tess. "It's a blessing. And you've blessed others all your life. That's part of what infuriates me. Who picks on people who make helping others a way of life? That makes no sense."

"Jerks?" Riley stood and hugged Gran. "Gotta go. Thank you for a wonderful supper. I've got to run figures for work first thing tomorrow, then I'll see what I can find online. I'm going to check into the donation site. We can lodge a formal complaint, but there's a terms-and-conditions page that no one ever reads. They just click 'I agree' as if they've read and considered every word. Including me, and I know better."

"I'll walk you out," said Tess. "Gran, do you need help with your pills?"

Gran shot Tess a look that made it clear she could handle taking three pills on her own, thank you very much. Gran headed to the sink while Tess walked out the front door with Riley.

Riley looked up. The almost-full moon had just crested the hills, and its welcome light brightened a starlit sky. "Nice moon."

"Oh. It is. It's gorgeous. There's always something so special about harvest moons."

"They seem bigger. Brighter."

She smiled. "Yes. When you're in Lower Manhattan you can see gorgeous sunrises if you go down to the seaport. But I realized how much I missed sunsets." The night had chilled, but then Riley slung an arm around her, and his warmth enveloped her. "I missed seeing the sun. Tall buildings and long days mean you rarely see the sun, and I realized last year that I missed being in the open. Being by the river. Feeling the north wind and seeing the waves and watching boats cruise back and forth. And I missed Gran. Our life here."

"So you came back."

"I was tired of money."

He whistled softly. "Not a phrase one hears very often."

It was one hundred percent truthful. She shrugged her shoulder. "I'd been working with it for nearly ten years. Moving it, making it, sheltering it, and stowing it. Working in investment banking is a lot like being the street hawker playing the cup game. You're always trying to figure out which cup covers the bean. And incorrect guesses are frowned upon."

"Did you have many of those, Tess?"

She shook her head. "I'm instinctively good. I made a crazy amount of money and had nothing to spend it on and no time to spend it, and I realized I'd turned into something I didn't like. But it's not easy to leave. And my bosses didn't make it any easier."

"Tempting you to stay?"

She laughed. "Threatening me with lawsuits if any clients follow me before the one-year no-competition clause is fulfilled."

"You're that good."

She smiled and for just a moment leaned her cheek against his sleeve. It was a soft cotton blend, like flannel only different. It felt nice. "I suppose. But coming here, helping Gran, chopping veggies and straining broths and proofing dough, has helped me so much. I'm calmer. Happier. Less aggravated."

"Content."

"Yeah." She leaned back and smiled up at him, and when she did, he leaned down.

She wasn't supposed to kiss him. She'd warned herself to hold back, maintain distance, stay cool.

When their lips met, the last thing she wanted was to maintain distance.

Her fingers tingled.

Her chest went tight, and her pulse jumped.

She wasn't sure who broke the kiss, because she was pretty sure neither one wanted that kiss to end, but when it did, he leaned his forehead against hers. "Well, then."

She stepped back. "Blame it on the moon, Mr. O'Toole."

"There was no moon this morning, or yesterday or the day before that, and I've been wondering what it would be like to kiss you since I walked into the soup shop last week. Now I know."

She should end this conversation right now. Take a firm step back and scold him roundly.

She didn't. She leaned back against his strong arm and met his gaze. "And?"

"Best kiss ever."

Good answer.

Great answer, actually. And when he winked and moved down the three steps, she wished he could stay. She wished he could take a seat on the stoop next to her and they could watch the moon do what moons do best. Shine on, for all to see. "I'll see you tomorrow, okay?"

She nodded. "Yes."

He reached back.

She reached out.

Their fingers touched briefly. And then he walked to his car, whistling softly.

She could get used to this.

Loving Riley. Being with him. Hearing that whistle come and go.

And while she knew it was impossible, didn't Gran always say that with God all things are possible? So why not this? Why not now? Her. Him.

Then Gran joined her on the step.

Gran wasn't going to leave Sleepy Hollow. She was an important part of the town, and her restaurant was an integral link between the historic village and the new upscale trend, because all kinds of people loved soup. Soup and bread had broad-based appeal.

Riley had a life in western New York. A good job. And if his mother sold the boat shop and moved away, she'd be safe and sound with Carrie and he'd be back in his suburban office outside of Rochester.

They'd both come back to the village to help people they loved, only his was a temporary transfer. Hers wasn't. And that was a reality check she took seriously.

Chapter Seven

Marita was normally a talker.

She wasn't a gossip, but the bright, middle-aged woman liked to chat while working. That was her norm.

But Marita Santiago had been unusually quiet since Granny June's collapse.

The quiet drove Tess crazy. She didn't want to be intrusive, but she broached the topic the next morning. "Marita? Is something wrong? Are you worried about Gran? Or your job? Because you needn't be. I'm not going anywhere, and we'll help Gran keep this place running. Okay?"

Marita turned her way. She was searing beef for Hannie's Beef & Barley Soup, a historic classic ranked number one on Gran's list. The annual "Sleepy Hollow's Best Soups" list was a real thing. Gran held a contest every January to see which soup was voted the annual favorite, and Hannie's Beef & Barley hit the top ten regularly.

This soup called for charbroiled beef. It was a tradition passed down by Tess's great-grandmother. Nadine Van Brunt had put together a collection of family recipes in the early nineteen hundreds, including favorites from the Van Brunt, Van Tassel, and Webb families. Hannie's Beef & Barley and her daughter's Hudson River Bean Stew withstood the test of time and made it to the chalkboard offerings on a regular basis between October and March.

Marita kept a close eye on the beef. It needed to be charred but not burnt, and the fire's heat made all the difference. "Gran told me about the money when I went to visit her in the hospital, Tess."

That was a relief. "I was hoping she would," Tess replied as she slid another tray of thick white Italian bread into the big oven. "It wasn't something I wanted to bring up here, and it was Gran's story to tell. Were you able to offer her any insight?"

Marita bit her lower lip. "Not insight. And I don't like talking bad about people. I wouldn't like it if someone did that about me or my family."

"Of course not."

"I didn't want to upset her recovery, but I've got to tell someone what I know."

Tess closed the oven door and leaned one hip against the butcher-block bread table. "I'm listening."

"I've noticed Don Postlewhaite hanging around the restaurant's Facebook page the last year-and-a-half."

"The nice guy that's worked at the post office forever?"

Marita winced. "Yes. Gran isn't one to bother much with social media, so I take care of the restaurant's page. I answer questions as Granny June's Soup Shop, and if I'm not sure about something, I run it by Gran. But because so many of the people are her friends on Facebook and have liked her restaurant page, sometimes they get mixed up and post stuff on the soup shop page that they should've posted on her personal page. Like the pet shelter stuff. I know what they talk about because some of those conversations end up on the shop page, and I know who's said what. Don never comments. Ever.

And yet, when he comes into the restaurant, he can pretty much quote what everyone's said."

"A lurker."

"Yes."

"Is that unusual for him? For anyone?" asked Tess. "I thought that's just what everybody does."

"Well, yes, but it's a good way to find information without people knowing you're doing it. It's amazing what you can discover. One of my favorite authors says she lurks on a few people's pages because they're so transparent on social media. She says she gets some of her best plot ideas that way." Eyes on the meat, she pursed her lips before she continued.

"I dug deeper after the money disappeared last week, and Don's been keeping an eye on at least sixteen people who donated. He's liked a lot of their posts—but again, he never comments. That's a lot of lurking and checking things out. I thought you should know."

"That's really helpful, Marita."

Marita used the wide spatula to flip the first batch of seared beef onto a platter, then filled the grill again. "Don's job was changed at the post office three years ago. They didn't call it a demotion, but he went from being a backroom sorter to a clerk, and that's a different pay grade. His granddaughter's been sick too. She's in remission right now, but she was in treatment for almost two years. She's lived with Don and Christina from the time she was in preschool and she's a teenager now." She seasoned the new beef strips, and the fire reacted with spurts of flame. "I'm not saying he did it. I'm just saying his behavior on Facebook is suspicious."

"I'll check it out," Tess promised. "Is that why you've been so quiet?"

"That. And wondering about my job. The soup shop. Gran."

"Well, put your mind at ease about the shop," Tess assured her. "I'm not the cook you are or the baker that Gran is, but I can hold my own proofing dough and baking bread while Gran recovers. And I can chop carrots and potatoes for hours." She exchanged a grin with Marita. "Being a soup sous chef might be my newest endeavor."

"Except you were making six figures in Manhattan." Marita scrunched up her face in disbelief. "That's a lot of money to walk away from."

"Not if you're unhappy and ridiculously lonely in a city of millions."

Marita's features softened. "It's like that sometimes, isn't it? Surrounded by people, yet completely alone. That was why we moved up here when I was a girl. The job situation was good before the plant closed, and the people in town were so friendly. Mama and I loved it. We didn't care that there were rich folks on the hill and we were barely making rent. We all went to the same churches, shared the same holidays, and sang the same hymns. It was wonderful. And so different than being in the city. Having my parents move here thirty-five years ago was a blessing, and when your grandmother brought me on board here, it just got better. But we weren't making the kind of money you were making, Tess. That's a lot to leave behind."

Tess paused the big mixer to add a touch more flour to the rolls. "It seemed like a hard decision for a long time, but once I made it, I was so relieved. All I could see was me growing old there, bossy and rich with a fancy upscale apartment, but not being with Gran or anyone I love. And I thought, what kind of life would that be?"

"You've got guts, Tess. I'm glad you're here. Especially now. God's timing is a wonderful thing."

"A year ago, I'd have rolled my eyes at that notion, but I don't roll my eyes anymore, because somehow or other I'm here at the right time."

"And Riley's here," added Marita. "I'm just sayin'."

Tess's cheeks warmed. "Well, that's most likely coincidence."

"Hmm." Marita didn't offer a verbal opinion, but the lack of one was an opinion in itself.

Tess pulled out her phone. "I'm going to see if Riley can check out Mr. Postlewhaite online."

"Online. The internet. The World Wide Web." Marita made quote marks with her fingers. "Remember when we used to call it that? So much has changed, but not this." She cast a fond look around the efficient and gleaming kitchen. "Not soup."

She was right.

Soup and bread withstood the sands of time. They were ageless. Timeless. Food of the ages and for the ages.

That thought made Tess smile, and when Riley sent back a hug GIF and a thumbs-up, her smile grew.

She wasn't good at flirtation. That had been Bridget's forte, not hers, but flirting with Riley wasn't just fun.

It was wonderful.

Chapter Eight

Don Postlewhaite had a pretty much nonexistent internet presence.

Other than a few less-than-stellar reviews of the local post office, the man had no hits on his name that weren't the usual pay-for-contact-info links. And Riley didn't see any reason to do that, since he could probably find out Don's address from his own mom.

Riley swung by the Sleepy Hollow Soup Shop midafternoon, thinking there would be a lull. But there was no lull. The sunlit day brought people to town in droves. They came to tour historic homes, walk the Sleepy Hollow Cemetery made famous in Irving's short story, and explore the RiverWalk and promenade. Senior citizen tour busses used St. Teresa's parking lot as a drop-off point. From there, tourists could stroll down Beekman to the river or wander the town. The hardier sort could navigate the hilly roads and make it up to the cemetery, but most of the tour buses added the cemetery and Kykuit, the Rockefeller mansion, to their stops for scheduled tours.

October in Sleepy Hollow wasn't anything like he remembered fifteen years before. The town's revitalization in tourism was one for the record books.

He parked in the church lot and started toward the cut-through leading to the soup shop.

Then he spotted Susan Mary. Again.

She slipped through the pass. She glanced right, then left.

Riley ducked back behind the privet hedge. The lack of trimming made it an easy and thick cover.

He pushed the hedge's center off-kilter slightly, just enough to see where she went.

She had a purse with a long shoulder strap. Both hands clutched one of those thick, soft, fluffy blankets that seemed to be everywhere the past few years. This one was in shades of blue with spots of white, like clouds against a deep blue sky.

She crossed the narrow alley and veered toward Beekman, just east of where he stood, but she never emerged onto the sidewalk.

He waited patiently for her to appear, and then not so patiently.

Had she spotted him? Was she on the other side of the boundary hedge, waiting for him to leave or move?

He took a chance and peeked around the corner.

Nothing.

The narrow pathway that led to the rear areas of the businesses facing Beekman was empty.

He grimaced, realizing she could have cut through the strip behind the businesses, emerged onto Cortlandt, and he wouldn't have been able to see it. So much for his detective skills.

He crossed the intersecting backyards and looked both ways when he came to Cortlandt. He didn't see her, and he'd lost time waiting. She could be anywhere by now.

He cut back through the yard, crossed the small parking area, and let himself into the soup shop kitchen just as Tess came through the swinging door. She had a stack of empty bread baskets and when she saw him, she didn't hesitate. "Hey, wash up, throw on some gloves, and load these up while I put the next batch into the oven, okay? Then I'll package the cooling ones. We've sold down to crumbs out there, and I'm putting out tomorrow's soup because we just sold out of today's."

The busyness of the shop reflected the onslaught of visitors. He was glad to help. "On it."

By the time he had the bread baskets full, Marita had joined them in the kitchen. "Sonya just got here from school. She's taking orders, I'll help you reload."

"Perfect. If Riley jumps in on packaging rolls, I'll start prep for tomorrow's soups."

The paper and plastic combo sleeves were an easy task, and there was something nice about having Tess working five feet away.

She grabbed fresh carrots, celery, onions, and potatoes and set them on her access table. "How did your research go?" She posed the question softly as she rinsed smudges of dirt from the celery sticks. "Did you discover anything about Mr. Postlewhaite?"

"Nope. Nothing." The rattle of the bag made him edge closer so she could hear him. "Cleanest internet presence ever."

"That could be suspicious in and of itself," said Tess. She took a spot at the prep table so she could face him.

He laughed. "It would be if he had a reason to be sanitized, but he doesn't. Other than financial stress three years ago, he's clear. Although his financial situation is still dicey," he admitted. "But he manages to stay afloat."

"Money is our motive though. So does that clear him? Or just move him down the list?"

Riley switched from Italian bread to sourdough. "Down the list. And from all reports he's a really nice guy, so I'm hoping he's not behind this. But I did see our accountant sneaking around again today. She slipped between Depeyster and Beekman, not far from the church. Carrying a blanket. Or two blankets."

Tess frowned. "Sneaking? Again?"

"As in furtive movements, glancing around, ducking down. Yep. Sneaking."

"But why?" muttered Tess as she chopped the carrots. "Why is she sneaking, and why did I dismiss her so quickly?"

"Because she seemed nice and normal and professional?" he suggested.

"I may have been duped," Tess admitted. "The love of flowers tipped her into the we-could-be-friends category…if I hadn't made her mad. But if she's creeping around, she's back on the list. The question is why?"

"Let's take a walk that way later."

"I'm in, as long as things are ready for tomorrow." She jutted her chin toward the front. "Marita and Sonya are visiting Gran for supper. She's making them a casserole. One of Marita's favorites, she said."

"I'll buy you supper while we explore."

She lifted her eyes.

Met his gaze. And when she did, it hit him again how much he liked locking eyes with her. Being with her. Spending time together.

But how could he make a commitment when his mother's situation was so precarious? If Doug's new assignment was in another part of the country, he and Carrie would be selling their newly renovated house and moving.

Would Mom move too?

So many questions and scant on answers. But when he was with Tess, the answers became possibilities. Possibilities that seemed brighter when she was a round. "Nothing fancy, mind you."

She laughed. "We'll save fancy for when we solve this mystery. It'll be our victory dance. Maybe that posh place up the hill."

"Maison Philipe? Deal."

It was after six by the time the next day's prep was done. Dark came earlier as the autumn daylight waned, but the village was well lit. He waited while she tested the lock, then they fell into step as they moved up Cortlandt.

The pedestrian traffic on Beekman was lighter, but vehicular traffic hadn't eased up. A lot of people came into town a day or two before the weekend. That gave them options of taking mansion tours before the weekend crowds descended on the small villages of Tarrytown and Sleepy Hollow. But locals coming home from work had to deal with the slow-moving traffic of visitors who jammed the GPS-directed routes to get where they were going.

The school playground was empty, and the combination police and fire department sat quietly, the big brick structure a sentinel overseeing the busy road.

"I can't imagine where she would have gone." Riley swept the street with a look right. Then left. "Anywhere, I guess."

"You didn't see her turn in either direction?"

He wished he'd checked around the bushes more quickly, but he hadn't. He shook his head. "I shouldn't have assumed she was taking a shortcut to Beekman. An unobtrusive one," he added.

Tess turned around. "Let's check the backs of the buildings."

"Dumpsters? See, Tess, this is why I like my kind of investigating. Click here. Click there. No dirty hands. No dumpster diving. No—"

"Riley. Look."

She reached for his hand. And for a moment, all that mattered was her hand in his. Her look of excitement when she nudged him to notice the back doors of a handful of businesses. He leaned down. "What am I looking for?"

"There are three small businesses with no front on Beekman, just a back-door access from here. Do you see it?"

He scanned the business names. Gordon's Tax & CPA Accounting, Pawfully Yours, and A Stitch in Time. "Got 'em. Not sure what to do with them."

"What was the major business near where you spotted her yesterday?"

"The vet clinic."

"And back here…"

"Oh, man." He got her drift. Paw prints pranced playfully across the small windows of Pawfully Yours. "A vet and a groomer. Now that's something to—"

A woman exited the pet groomer's. She wore scrubs covered with frolicking puppies, and the scent of dog shampoo wafted from the shop as she came their way.

Tess moved forward. "Ma'am? Is this your shop?" She pointed to the grooming salon, then the scrubs. "Of course, it is. The scrubs," she added, as if putting two and two together. "I think a woman I know was here earlier."

"Yes?"

She pointed to Riley. "We've talked about what it would be like to have a dog, but I don't like to go into anything without a plan, so maybe you can help us. If my friend was here, then I know you must know your stuff."

"Who was your friend?"

"More of an acquaintance," confessed Tess. "Susan Mary—"

"Oh, of course!" The woman smiled, delighted to talk about dogs and her business. "She brought in the little rescue pooch that needed a full-on treatment. She's a mini goldendoodle."

Riley offered her an encouraging smile, glad that HIPAA privacy rules didn't apply to pets.

"She said the owner fell ill and no one realized that Pippi wasn't being looked after. That dog has fallen into good fortune now, let me tell you, because Susan Mary was absolutely doting on her."

"I love a good-hearted dog story," declared Riley. "So you do all breeds?"

"Most," she told him. "Were you thinking a particular breed? Or a shelter dog?"

"We're not sure," said Tess, and she was right, but the thought of Tess and him and a dog of their own painted a picture he hadn't considered before. A picture he liked. "But we appreciate the information. And it's so nice to meet you."

"You too. Here's my card." The woman pulled a business card out of her pocket. "Give me a call if you need a groomer. We're always happy to meet new clients. Like Pippi. What a nice little dog she is and so blessed to have such a loving owner."

They went one way.

The groomer went the other.

And when they were out of earshot, Tess grabbed his arm. "Susan Mary was sneaking around with a dog!"

"So it would seem."

"But why sneak?" Tess asked. "Could she be that embarrassed by what she said on Facebook?"

"With good reason," Riley told her. The night air was chilling quickly. "She was adamant about the group's misdirected focus. So coming up with a rescue dog a few weeks later is a real turnaround, right?"

"It sure is. I don't know if that puts her higher on the list or lower. But it makes me rethink her lack of heart for animals."

"Whereas I think better on a full stomach. Come on." He slipped off his jacket and put it over her shoulders. "There's a warm Irish pub waiting to serve us great food."

"Waiting could be the operative term," she told him, but when they got to Doyle's, they were seated within five minutes. She angled an appreciative expression his way. "You either have pull or you slipped the hostess a significant tip."

He laughed. "Neither. Parties of two are easier to seat. Simple math."

That's what he said, but there was nothing simple about this. Any of this. Gran's health crisis, the missing money, the angry neighbor. At the moment, it felt like they'd spent five days spinning their wheels with nothing to show for it.

But sitting here with Riley seemed simply right.

They enjoyed a wonderful supper, and when they walked back to their respective cars, he took her hand again.

The weather had changed while they were having dinner. The brisk wind and chilling air had chased a lot of people inside. The trees danced in the wind, scattering yellow leaves here and there, but the thick-trunked maples were still in full leaf. The branches whispered and whistled above them and, between the branches, a break in the clouds revealed the almost-full moon. It peeked through with a shimmering aura, as if checking things out before a band of swift-moving dark clouds danced across its surface.

"Well?" He faced her.

She faced him. And when his eyes posed a question, her smile offered an answer.

He drew her into his arms. It wasn't just the strength of his embrace that felt good, it was the warmth. The caring. He glanced down at her lips.

She reached up, easing the distance.

And then she stopped. "Do you smell smoke?"

He grimaced. "I'd make a joke about sizzling romance, but I do, actually." He let go of her and turned. His height gave him an advantage, but when the clouds broke again, Tess caught a glimpse of a dark cloud of smoke.

And it was coming from the Sleepy Hollow Soup Shop.

CHAPTER NINE

The fire department's response team got to the fire at the same time they did.

It wasn't the restaurant burning.

It was the dumpster in the parking area behind the restaurant. Horrible fumes filled what had been clean, crisp night air.

The upstairs tenants had seen the fire and called it in. They had moved their cars out of the danger zone, giving the firefighters a straight shot at fighting the fire.

Gran called Tess within two minutes. "There's a fire? I heard it come across the scanner, Tess. What's happened? What's going on? Are you all right?"

She'd forgotten that Gran liked to have the scanner on when she was home alone. She claimed she wasn't a bit nosy. Simply concerned about the well-being of her hometown. But Tess was pretty sure there was a dash of nosy mixed in with the genuine concern. She'd unlocked the restaurant's front door, turned on the lights, and double-checked the soup shop. All good. "It's all right, Gran. Riley and I are both fine, and it's not the restaurant. It's the dumpster. It kind of exploded into flames about ten minutes ago. At least that's when the upstairs renters noticed it."

"There's nothing that goes into that dumpster that goes up in flames like that, darling girl. Smolder, yes. But that's what they said? 'Exploded into flames'?"

"They were watching TV and suddenly there was a big, bright orange flash outside their back window. They looked out, the dumpster was on fire, and they called it in. We were just on our way home after grabbing supper at Doyle's."

Gran loved Doyle's. She'd been a loyal customer of theirs for years. "Their dumplings are the best comfort food on the planet. Next to soup and bread, that is."

"Agreed."

"Should I have Marita bring me down? Tell me exactly what's going on, Tessie."

"You stay home and follow doctor's orders." Tess kept her voice firm. "It's a dumpster fire, no more, no less, and they've put it out. Right now they're talking with people and making sure there aren't any live embers."

"And no one was hurt?"

"Not a scratch. I'll be home in a few minutes, Gran."

Gran didn't cede control easily. She never had. But this time she sighed softly. "I'll stay put."

The note of resignation hit Tess hard.

Gran wasn't young. The heart episode drove that realization home.

But she was still sharper than many young executives Tess knew. Sidelining her seemed wrong.

Riley touched her shoulder. "Let's get back to her house. Our presence will assure her that everything's fine here."

"All right." Tess thanked the tenant again. She and Riley crossed the small lot. The fire chief met them halfway. "We're going to cordon off this area for a day, Tess."

Tess frowned. "Residual heat?"

The assistant fire chief joined them. "There's evidence of an accelerant."

"Arson?" Riley looped an arm around Tess's shoulders. "Are you sure?"

The fire chief nodded. "We'll follow up with some testing, but why would anyone want to light up Gran's dumpster?"

Tess and Riley exchanged looks. Tess wasn't sure what to say.

The assistant chief grimaced. "The pet fund, eh? You think someone's mad at Gran for losing their money?"

"You know about that?"

"Small town, Tess. Most of us know. You think someone is out to get Gran on account of the money? That's harsh when she lost a chunk herself."

"It sure is," said Tess, but his words had sparked her brain in a different direction. "Or someone is warning us off because we're getting too close."

"Gran never put cameras back here?"

Tess shook her head. "No."

"Might be something you want to consider moving forward," said the chief. "That little dead space is virtually unseen, and there've been a couple of incidents there this year."

"I'll take care of it," Tess told him.

"It's a good move. We'll be in touch."

She and Riley cut through the church property to the parking lot.

Thickening clouds had obscured the moon, but the trees still danced in the autumn wind.

She got into her car.

He climbed into his and they drove back to Gran's place. They parked in the driveway, and Gran met them at the door.

She wasn't worried. She wasn't scared. She was in full battle-ready mode. She gave them a good looking over to make sure they were fine, then crossed her arms and tapped her foot. "I've owned that place for nearly forty years and we've never once had a dumpster fire, so you know what that means, don't you?"

Tess peeled off her sweater and set it on the nearest chair. "Either burning rolls will be our eventual downfall or someone is issuing us a warning?"

Gran pressed her lips into a line and nodded. "Exactly. You're getting close. Rattling cages, even if you can't see the answer quite yet. Someone's worried. Worried enough to threaten without harm, if you know what I mean." She directed her attention to Riley. "I got my invite to that group you set up," she said. "It's a good idea because now we can share information and he or she won't know what's happening."

"That's the plan," said Riley, but when Gran went off to answer her ringing phone in the kitchen, he said to Tess, "Except I'm pretty sure whoever did this is part of the group. The inner circle of friends and pet lovers. There was enough information in the media posts to make them a prime target for a bleeding-heart nonprofit. All the thief had to do was pick a plausible name, sponsor a few ads, and then innocently share the ads."

"Which drew them in."

He nodded. "Don't mention this to Gran. I don't want her suspicious of all her friends. We'll keep it steady on the home front and paw through things behind the scenes." He grinned. "Pun intended."

Then he looked down again.

At her mouth.

She scolded him with a look. "Don't be starting something we can't finish, O'Toole."

"Who says we can't finish, Tess?"

She leaned her forehead against his chest for just a moment. "You'll be leaving after Christmas. I'll be staying here. You'll be chasing cyber bad guys in Rochester or wherever your mom ends up. I'll be helping Gran. Maybe we should—"

He didn't let her finish.

He tipped her chin up and kissed her.

It was perfect. Wonderful. The best kiss ever. The only downside was the short duration. Because she'd have liked to go on kissing him, say... forever?

When he was done, he drew her in for a big hug. "I'm not sure what November and December will bring, but the more time we spend together, the more I realize what I truly want, Tess." He gave her a frank look. "And that means more than anything."

Oh, her heart.

It didn't just pitter-pat in her chest. It raced. Because maybe— just maybe— it would all work out.

Chapter Ten

"I've got an offer of 2.1 million dollars on the table for B&K Boats and Marina."

Riley whistled softly as his mother read the rest of the email from the local Realtor. "'My guess is that the offer will climb. With the enthusiasm for the Edge-on-Hudson development, this was a no-brainer. No pressure. Just wanted you to know that interest is rising.'"

His mom sighed and set the printout on the table. "More like the wolves are circling." She sat down hard in a chair and pointed to the countertop behind Riley. "Coffee."

"On it." He poured a cup for each of them and brought them to the table. "Does Carrie know?"

His mother shook her head. "No. I was busy getting the kids to school and didn't open the email until I got back here. Millions, Riley." She sipped the coffee. "Your dad and I used to joke about the rise in land values, but we never thought this." She aimed a look at the paper on the table. "That's preposterous money to people like us."

"It's a game-changer," he acknowledged. "That's *if* you want to change the game," he went on. "We don't know what Carrie and Doug will be doing yet, but if he gets a promotion to the Dallas office, they might just take it. He's not a fan of winter or taxes."

His mother made a wry face. "And we've got plenty of both up here."

"We sure do." Riley slid into the chair next to her. "Do you want to entertain the idea of staying if they're gone?"

She stood and paced the floor. Then she crossed to the window and stared out. Another brilliant October day had erupted with bright sun, colorful flowers, and changing leaves. "I don't know. I want to be part of my grandchildren's lives. I don't want to be an absentee grandma. Your dad and I never considered being snowbirds, although we did like getting away for a couple of weeks now and again. But this." She stared at the letter on the table. "It's different now, because he's gone."

"I know." Riley stayed where he was, letting her talk. She didn't need his opinion. She needed his love and support.

"If it were five or ten years later and your dad was here, we'd probably jump at the chance and do some traveling, then leave the bulk to you and your sister."

"We're not hurting for money, Mom. Either of us. Spend it all."

"I'm not like that."

She wasn't. Never had been.

A frown drew her brows down. "I've never been a big fan of leisure, I don't like aimless expenditures, and I don't like spending on myself. So why leave? Why sell? But practically speaking, can I run the business on my own?" She drew a breath and shrugged. "No. It's a two-person operation that goes to three or four in the summer to help with rentals and boat checks."

"There are lots of people available to hire, Mom. College kids home in May. Retirees looking to work part-time. It's always worked out."

"Yes. I'm not sure what I'll do if Carrie and Doug end up moving away, but I can't wait for spring to make up my mind." A pensive note deepened her tone. "A buyer would need time to transfer things and get ready for the spring influx. Running a marina isn't for the faint of heart."

Riley started to say something, then stopped.

She thought the buyer would buy the business and keep it a boat shop.

Riley knew better.

B&K Boats and Marina would be history within weeks of her signing the purchase offer. The property was worth more than the two million-plus offered. The boats alone were a cool million, but he didn't have to explain all that now. She was openly discussing things for the first time in the nearly seven months since his father passed away, and that was good. He stood and wrapped her in a hug. "Don't rush things. That's what you told me at the cemetery in March. That you didn't intend to jump into anything. I'd grab hold of that thought. You had a great financial year. It's okay to breathe a little."

"And if they take the offer back?" she asked, ever practical. "And I've missed my chance?"

"You read what the Realtor said. They'll follow it up with a bigger and better one, Mom. Or someone else will. They can't make more land. You've got a beautiful slice of riverfront property that you and Dad bought when the town was still North Tarrytown and the street signs were white." The town had changed the street signs to a Washington Irving-friendly black on orange as part of their re-imaging for tourism, and visitors loved the change. "Everything was cheaper then. This is your investment paying off. And if Carrie and Doug move away, you've got three choices." He held up one finger. "Follow them."

She nodded.

He waggled a second finger. "Kidnap the kids and keep them here."

That made her smile.

He waved the third finger. "Or use that six months when your presence here isn't required and go visit them, then come back and run your business. You could have a place by them for winter, and they'd have a place to visit in the summer. It's something to think about," he finished as he tugged his jacket into place. "You're not in a corner, Mom. You've got lots of options. And time to consider them. Okay?"

"You've always known how to look at the heart of a situation," his mother replied. She stood, reached out, and gave him a hug. "That's what makes you so good at what you do. You know how to look behind the scenes. Yes. I'll take time to think, like you suggested. And breathe."

Something she said triggered his brain.

Behind the scenes.

It clicked.

He returned the hug. "Gotta go. I just thought of something I want to check out, but I'm meeting Tess down at the post office first. See you later. Okay?"

"Agreed."

The small post office was on Beekman, a ten-minute walk from his mother's place and five minutes from the Sleepy Hollow Soup Shop. He threaded his way through tourist traffic and got to the post office just as Tess rounded the corner from Cortlandt.

Simply beautiful.

Tess wasn't just girl-next-door pretty. She was amazing. Bright. Witty. Brilliant.

She spotted him and smiled.

That smile inspired him to halve the distance between them because waiting for her to get to him would take too long. Way too long. And that was a truth that made him want to smile back.

"Good morning, Mr. Postlewhaite."

The quaint post office was empty, and Tess approached the counter, Riley behind her. "You're working the front end now?" she asked in a conversational tone.

He smiled when he recognized her. "Tess McIntosh, I heard you were back. My Jeanne picked up soup and rolls two days ago, and she said that you were there and how nice it was to see you."

"It was good to see her too." She beamed at him, then felt bad for doing so because she was there to investigate him and right now that felt wrong. "I love being back. And helping Gran."

"Fortuitous timing there," he said. "Your grandmother is salt of the earth, and I hate even thinking about anyone causing her trouble. Goes against everything this town stands for. And then her getting sick, besides." He frowned. "Me and Jeanne, we know our share of that, and your grandmother has been good to us. Quite good." He ran his hand through his thinning hair. "She's a blessing."

Was he sincere?

Or was this a well-done one-act play for their benefit, to throw them off?

"She gave us a scare, that's for sure. Having so many people lose money in the pet fund scheme was a blow to her because she'd never take advantage of people."

"Got that straight." Don's tone was firm. "There are scammers everywhere these days. Phone. Mail. Online. It pays to be vigilant, but I saw those pictures and posters, and you'd have to be heartless to scroll on by."

"Were you one of the donors?" asked Riley.

Mr. Postlewhaite shook his head as Tess handed him a small package over the counter. "No. We've had our share of medical bills, and that's meant less giving. I love dogs well enough, but my granddaughter is my pride and joy, so we've given up this, that, and the other thing lately. A pot of soup is just as good as fancy stuff, and all that matters is that she's in remission. So far, so good, and they say if we get to five years of N.E.D.—"

He saw Tess's confusion and explained. "No evidence of disease. You learn a lot of cancer talk when you're living it."

"We're on year three," he added as he typed the address on the package into his system. "By the time she's done with high school, we'll know more, so Jeanne and I just keep facing forward. With prayers and good times. Just in case."

Oh, her heart... The thought of these good people facing a life-threatening illness with their only grandchild. "I'll join that prayer group, Mr. P."

"I'd be grateful. That's seven dollars and eighty-two cents, Tess."

She swiped her card, and when she and Riley were back on the street, she pulled out her phone and deleted Don from her suspect list. "No way he's involved. Agreed?" She looked up at Riley.

"One hundred percent. I'm going to walk you back to the shop, and then I'm heading home to follow up on something."

"Something you're ready to share?"

He shook his head, but she didn't miss the glimmer in his eye, as if he knew something she didn't. "Not yet. It came to me this morning when my mom talked about what goes on behind the scenes. And if we've got all or most of the donors on that spreadsheet, I want to see who was there but behind the scenes."

"Least obvious."

"Exactly. I'll text you when I'm free, okay? And if you need help at the restaurant, I'll come by later."

She didn't stop to think about where they were or who might see what or that in a small town, news traveled fast.

She reached out and hugged him. And she wasn't in any big hurry to let go either. Then she stepped back. "Thank you. I couldn't have done this alone. Not the restaurant, Gran's heart episode, the theft, checking things out. I'm not just glad Gran called you. I'm awfully glad you're here."

"Gran would call that a 'God-gift.'"

Tess smiled up at him. "I'm inclined to agree. See you later."

"Countin' the minutes, ma'am."

He was flirting with her.

She was flirting with him. And a few minutes later, as she got busy mixing dough in the bright, shiny kitchen, the thought of a lifetime of those flirtations seemed wonderful.

It probably couldn't happen. She knew that. But a girl was allowed to dream, and Tess hadn't indulged in dreams of ever-after in a long time.

Today she did.

Chapter Eleven

Riley jogged back to the townhouse.

After he scoured social media accounts, the spreadsheet, and what he could see in the donation's web pages, he sat back.

The little dog he'd seen on Beekman. That little smushed-face critter that turned out to be a French bulldog, an insanely expensive breed. And the man in the beret at the other end of the leash.

Riley remembered where he'd seen him now. He'd been at Gran's house three days ago at that meeting. He was one of the donors. Not a big one. But there, in the background.

Behind the scenes.

He pulled up the man's profile. The man and Gran weren't friends on Facebook, so his view was limited, but when he checked further, there was a business page attached for public view. He clicked on the page.

Maison Philipe.

This guy owned the high-end restaurant on Hobb's Hill, overlooking the river. The fancy place with the pricey dessert that the owner had dropped off to Gran as a get-well gift.

He pulled up the restaurant's photo history, and there was that little dog, looking like a mix of pug and bulldog that had gone through a shrinking machine. And there was a picture of the restaurant owner, Philip Marsten Rossiter, wearing a Paris-friendly cap and holding the dog.

in Sleepy Hollow, New York

Philip Marsten Rossiter was the man behind the scam.

Why would he want to hurt Gran and her friends?

Money, of course. In the end, it always came down to money.

Now it was his turn to look behind the scenes. What he found confirmed his suspicions. Philip Rossiter was in a major financial crisis. He'd been late on tax payments the last two years and hadn't paid the current ones yet. His credit rating had been flagged over a year ago with a score so low that no one would sign off on a loan for him.

Riley texted Tess that he needed to see her that night. I'LL BRING SUPPER. NO. WAIT. LET GRAN COOK. I'LL BRING DESSERT.

She texted him back immediately. YES. AFTER SIX. CRAZY BUSY HERE. HELP WANTED.

He laughed. SEE YOU IN AN HOUR. He finished his search, locked in data, and headed to the bakery to grab dessert. It wouldn't be French. But if he had to accuse one of Gran's friends, he wanted to ease the revelation with a great dessert.

The fact that a fruit-and-chocolate layered cake would make Tess happy was just an added bonus.

His phone rang on the way to the bakery.

He answered it and stopped to listen, right there in the street.

Darrowfield Incorporated, one of the biggest internet tech safety firms, was reaching out to him, offering him the chief of operations officer position in their Florida office. "We don't have the restrictions you have up there, Riley," said Brian Darrow, the mastermind behind the company. Brian was on the cutting edge of the IT industry at its inception, and his company had grown along with the internet. The guy was worth mega millions. "You know your stuff. And you were at RIT when our current COO was there. He thought highly of you then, and he's been watching your career. He knows you're a rising star. You don't just chase a trail. You insert blocks to make the trails go astray or leave a mark, and that's cutting-edge stuff. Think about it," he added. "I don't need an answer for a few weeks, but I want my next year's staff locked in by Thanksgiving."

James Hadley had been one of most intuitive technical instructors Riley had ever met. He'd been fortunate to be at Rochester Institute of Technology when Hadley was a professor there. "Why is James leaving?" he asked. "He's not old."

"No, but his wife is ill. They're going to Texas for treatments. Understandably, he wants to focus his time on her."

Another one of life's left turns, but James Hadley had the resources and the options to change his life dramatically to save his wife. Most people didn't have those choices. "Brian, I'm honored—"

"I sense a 'but,' so I'm going to stop you right there," said Darrow. "Consider the offer. I'll send you a deal memo with terms. We're in full-on office mode down here and we only do remote as needed, so it would require relocating. But if you don't mind perennial summer, Florida is a great place to be."

He loved Florida. It was a great place. And when winter rolled its long, cold Arctic fingers across Western New York, the thought of daily warmth had crossed his mind more than once. "I'll be in touch."

The deal memo came almost instantly. He opened the email. Scanned the numbers and terms. Then he whistled softly.

He'd been happy with the paycheck Centurion deposited into his account every two weeks.

in Sleepy Hollow, New York

This offer could make him four times as happy.

Except he didn't need four times the money. Did he?

The fact there was no state tax in Florida added another bonus to an already great offer.

He put the phone back in his pocket.

His father gone. His mother's options. His sister's possible move. And Tess here, in Sleepy Hollow, to help Gran. A mystery to solve, and now—

The job offer of a lifetime.

A job that didn't just change his location and income. It elevated him to a level of respect within an industry that harbored few giants.

Was that his goal? Had that ever been his goal?

No.

And yet, having that opportunity dangled in front of him was a true temptation. It was the opportunity to skip six rungs of a ten-rung ladder.

The smell of fresh bread welcomed him into the Sleepy Hollow Soup Shop.

Tess turned when the door clicked open. "Riley!" She waggled a clutch of carrots she was rinsing in the big white sink. "Enter if you dare, and pick your poison, sir." She pointed to the right and then to her carrots. "Bread and roll detail or veggie prep? Two wonderful options for passing the time of day."

"Veggies." He washed up, grabbed an apron, and relieved her of carrot duty. "If the coming and going from the church parking lot is an indicator, the weekend is going to be crazy, Tess. How can I help you get ready for it? And how does the church keep people from filling the lot on Sunday morning?"

"I'm not sure about the latter question, but I'll let them handle that. And you're already helping by getting veggie prep done," she assured him. "I'm coming in at four—"

"In the morning?" He didn't try to mask the note of horror in his tone.

She laughed. "Yes. Marita's coming in at five and Sonya at eight. We'll have everything stocked, and we'll have replacement soups prepared for midday changes as needed. Gran's got half a dozen make-ahead soups that don't lose flavor or texture by sitting overnight, so we'll put those in the warmers first thing in the morning to be replenished with fresh pots when those run low. And Marita says they will, by one o'clock."

"That's a lot of soup in three hours."

"If last weekend was an indicator, we'll still run out. I promised Gran that we'll keep her apprised, but when she worried about the extra hours I'm working, I reminded her that Wall Street isn't exactly nine-to-five, even if the markets are closed. Oddly, that made her feel better."

"Do you miss it, Tess?"

There was no hesitation in her reply as she floured the board before she worked the dough. "No. I thought I would, but no. It owned me. Partially my fault for allowing it, but also because it's expected, and I tend to rise to expectation."

"So you came back." Peeling and dicing fifteen pounds of carrots offered the perfect time to pry.

"Not because of that."

He lifted an eyebrow.

"I was getting disenchanted, yes, but then I ran into a man downtown. One of the first nice days we had last spring after a tough winter. A beautiful day, first week of April. Everyone and his brother came out of their offices to grab lunch because the weather had been cold, wet, rainy, and dreary for so long. Anyway, there was this man. An older guy, well past retirement age. His coat was on fire."

Riley stopped peeling.

"No flames," she said. She kept working the dough, but he didn't miss the intensity of her expression. "Not yet, but clouds of smoke were coming from his coat. He stood there, on Maiden Lane, looking confused and lost. People were sending him all kinds of looks, but no one stopped to help him."

"Except you."

Chin down, she nodded. "We got the jacket off. It turned out to be his pocket that was burning. He'd tried to save a cigarette butt for later in the day, but it wasn't quite out. I tore the pocket away, and he was so grateful, Riley. For just that little bit of help, so grateful. That's when I realized I was a fish out of water." She began cutting the rolls and placing them on the tray. "I didn't want to be that person who walked by, ever. And I didn't want to be where that kind of reaction was the norm. Of course, changing locations is easy to do when you've made a lot of money. A lot of people don't have choices like that. I did. And I couldn't be happier."

"Really?" When she looked up, he winked. "There's nothing else in town that could add to that happiness, Tess? I might find that insulting."

She laughed. "I think we've already established that your presence is appreciated by me and Gran. And your mom. She'll miss you when you go back, Riley."

"And you, Tess?" He wanted to hear her say it. That she'd miss him. Maybe that she didn't want him to go. But she rolled her eyes at him and pointed a flour-dusted finger his way.

"Who wouldn't miss free help, O'Toole?"

He faked a frown, and that made her laugh. Then she sighed. "I'm lamenting our timing, for sure. Because I absolutely, positively would like to get to know you better. But my job, my life, my work is here, helping Gran. I can't deny that it feels good to be helping someone again." She raised a slice of dough into the air before setting it in the pan. "I'm working for a good cause and not lining rich people's pockets. There's a lot of satisfaction in soup."

"I concur."

By the time they were done prepping and had everything clean, it was six thirty.

"Gran made pot roast," said Tess as she locked the back door. Riley tossed a pair of bags into the cleaned-out dumpster.

"My favorite. That and beef stew."

"Now that's some down-home cooking."

"My mom's a real Yankee at heart, even though she moved here from Chesapeake Bay. Her dad ran a boat business there, so she brought a lot of information to the table when she and Dad opened B&K Marina. My dad loved boats and she loved him, so they combined their talents and managed to stay in love and work together for nearly forty years. That's pretty impressive, right?"

"It is. My parents drifted apart when the plant closed, and if it hadn't been for Gran and Gramps, Bridget and I would have ended up as carry-on bags for Mom's flights of fancy after Dad passed away. That's what we called her boyfriends," she explained. "Finally,

Gran suggested we finish high school with her and Gramps, and Mom was on the next flight to some cool new development in Arizona. And that was that."

"You never see her?"

Tess shrugged. "I've flown down a couple of times. She's busy. She has a life there, it's different. Let's just say her current photo status is a selfie. Not a family print done at the local mall. Bridget stopped visiting about five years ago, when she had Brandon. I think she figured if Mom wanted to see him, she'd come up. That never happened."

"I'm sorry, Tess." They'd arrived at their cars, parked on the far side of the church lot. "That hurts."

"It did, but it taught me a good lesson." She reached for the door handle, but he was faster. He swung the door open for her. "It made me realize that sacrificial love is a wonderful thing. Like Gran and Gramps. And your family, Riley. It taught me to think less about myself and more about others, and when I saw that old man needing help, I realized that the city is a great place to establish credentials, but it isn't for me long-term. I'd misplaced the lessons I'd learned years before, and I wanted to get a grasp on them again." She tipped her gaze up to his, a gaze full of trust and hope. "You said you've got news for Gran?"

"I think I've found our thief, Tess."

"Seriously?" She grabbed the front of his jacket with both hands. "Who?"

He put his hands over hers. Gazed into her deep brown eyes. And then he laughed. "Supper first. Then I'll show you and Gran what I found. Did you remember the bread?" Gran had asked them to bring home a loaf of crusty Italian.

Tess nodded to her bag. "Sure did. Don't change the subject. Who is it, Riley?"

She'd remembered the bread.

He'd forgotten dessert. The phone call had derailed him.

He backpedaled toward Cortlandt and the popular bakery. "Way easier to explain it once to both of you. I'll see you in ten minutes. Okay?"

She skewered him with a frown but nodded.

She wasn't afraid to tease him or rattle him or make him think.

He loved that about her. In fact, there wasn't much he didn't love about Tess, but was it crazy to fall head over heels with someone in such a short time?

Crazy but nice.

Falling for Tess added a whole new element to his options list, and he was sure of one thing. Tess McIntosh was at the top of that list.

Chapter Twelve

"Philip Rossiter?" Gran's eyes went wide, but her jaw tightened as her lips formed a thin, straight line. "I should have known."

"How?" asked Tess because Riley hadn't explained his reasoning yet.

"French onion soup!" declared Gran, fuming. When she saw their confused looks, she went on. "We held a fundraiser in April when we all got on board with the charity. A bunch of local businesses donated food for a potluck. We held it in the church parking lot, and Philip did a monster-sized pot of French onion soup. That should have been my clue, but then he was always frugal, for all his show-off ways."

"I'm still confused," said Riley.

"Broth and onions," said Gran. "That's how you make French onion soup. Then a slice of bread, which I made, and cheese on top. The cheese was donated from Donofrio's Deli. I never even gave it a thought then because it was such good soup. Better than mine, even, but it's a very inexpensive recipe to make. To think Philip scammed us from within is an awful thing. I don't consider everyone in the group a friend, but we're all looking out for this town. Why would anyone do that?"

"Money," said Tess.

"Money," agreed Riley. "He's in financial trouble. Behind on everything. Probably figured this was an easy way to get out of debt."

"By stealing?"

Tess winced but nodded. "Yes. It's a tale as old as time, Gran. Grand scale or small scale. Stealing is stealing."

"And he may have started small and got himself hooked when he saw how easy it was," suggested Riley.

"We made it easy," Gran shot back.

"He made it inviting," Riley corrected her. "This isn't your fault. Not yours or any of the donors. You saw and believed, so you gave. Now we need to confront Philip and get that money back. If it's there."

"Not tonight," Gran said firmly.

Riley frowned. "Why?"

"Because everyone in the restaurant biz knows that a good Friday night makes or breaks the week, and if money's that tight, no sense in making it worse. I can make his life miserable in the morning."

"Gran, you've got the best heart." Tess hugged her. "Riley, can you go with Gran to Maison Philipe tomorrow morning?"

"Let's go to his house instead," Gran said. "It's just beyond the hill, about five minutes north."

Riley nodded. "I'll pick you up at nine. All right?"

"Nine it is. Tess, are you and Marita all right with the restaurant tomorrow?"

"Yes, ma'am." Tess slung an arm around Gran's shoulders. "Locked and loaded. Will you two be all right talking to Philip? We could simply give the information to the police. Let them take it from here."

"And give Philip more time to spend the money?" Gran's chin came up. She crossed her arms again, and the last thing Tess wanted was to get her upset. "Our officers will be insanely busy the next few days with people coming to spend the weekend here. And for all Philip's hoity-toity ways, he's generally an okay guy. He's helped a lot of folks over the years. Riley, you're sure of your facts on this?"

Riley took a picture out of the folder he'd brought with him. "The scammer used this picture of a French bulldog as his second round of defense in account recognition."

"Pierre!" Gran may have given Philip the benefit of doubt before, but the little dog's picture nailed him. "Oh, Philip. What have you done?"

"We'll find out, first thing," promised Riley. He stood and set his empty plate on the old-fashioned countertop. "I'll see you in the morning, Gran."

"I'll set my things out now so I'm ready."

She moved to the stairs while Tess walked Riley to the door. He turned her way before leaving. "Do you think this is too much of a shock for her?"

"For Gran?" She sent him a look of disbelief.

"I mean with her heart and all. I could just go and confront the guy myself."

Tess shook her head. "Gran would never sit back and let things go, and they said her heart's fine now that they've done the procedure. They gave her the all clear as long as she follows directions. And she will. No, let her come along. She's known Mr. Rossiter for a long time. Not friends, maybe, but she liked to think of him as a fellow local restaurateur."

"He did call the soup shop a soup kitchen," Riley reminded her. "That's less than friendly."

"He's pretentious and somewhat obnoxious, but like Gran said, he's done a lot of good for the hollow and some local people."

Riley wrapped her in a hug, a hug she'd like to enjoy for a long time to come. That wasn't possible, so she'd take what she could get right now. "Good luck with that early wake-up call," he said.

"Good luck with Philip. And let me know what's happening, all right?"

"I will. And Tess?"

"Mm-hmm?"

She looked up.

He looked down. His gaze settled on her lips, and for a sweet, sweet moment, she thought he was going to kiss her again.

He did.

On the forehead. Like you'd kiss an old friend goodbye.

And then he left, leaving mixed messages in his wake. If there was one thing Tess had learned in investment banking, it was that if a client gave off mixed messages, it was because he or she was second-guessing their relationship with the firm and her.

She was pretty sure the same held true in romance.

Chapter Thirteen

Tess sent Riley and Gran a picture of a bread rack full of loaves bagged and labeled, ready to go once the midday rush hit. WE'VE GOT THIS COVERED, she texted. SIX POTS OF SOUP IN COOLER AS BACKUP. THINKING OF YOU BOTH THIS MORNING!

She didn't add anything personal.

But then, he didn't deserve personal after walking away last night.

Riley didn't waffle as a rule. He was a straight-shooting, follow-the-facts kind of man, but right now he felt like he was in one of those pick-your-own-ending books, except the choices weren't solely up to him. Not when it came to his mother and her future.

Gran hurried out to the car as soon as he hit the driveway. They pulled up outside Philip Rossiter's small home a few minutes later.

They converged on the front door and rang the bell.

No one answered.

Rossiter had one of those camera doorbells, so Riley looked straight into it and spoke. "Philip, we've come to talk to you. Open up."

The funny little dog—Pierre—growled and leaped at the door. He perched on a table drawn up to the front window and went into small-dog-style apoplexy because they were on his turf.

And still no Philip.

"Let's check the restaurant." Gran marched back to the car, determined. Riley followed at an easier pace, but when they pulled into the parking lot of Maison Philipe two minutes later, there were two cars parked there. He reached out and put a hand on her arm. "If you get too upset, I'll have to do this alone. Your granddaughter would never forgive me if I let something happen to you."

"I can't help being upset that someone who presented himself as almost a friend, who deliberately joined forces with us, is the conspirator who stole our money. But I'm fine, Riley," she said firmly. "Just fine. The doctors fixed the problem quite nicely with their little balloon trick, and I feel great. But I'm also understandably perturbed, so if you won't let me in on this, I'll just get in my car at home and go it alone."

"Clearly Tess gets her stubbornness from you."

Gran smiled. "She's got a lot of me in her, no doubt. You ready?"

He swung the car door open. "Let's do it."

The front door of the restaurant was locked. They didn't open until eleven. Riley and Gran headed for the kitchen access.

Two men were inside, busy with chopping and stirring. The older of the two turned when they came in, his look expectant.

And then his face fell. "You aren't Philip."

"No, but we're looking for him," said Riley.

"Aren't we all?" The man frowned. "I don't have the proper cuts of meat in the freezer or cooler, our seafood order hasn't arrived, and it seems our produce order was canceled. How am I supposed to get things ready for a busy October weekend when I have so few supplies? Philip isn't here, he isn't answering his phone, he's completely abandoned us in our hour of need. What am I supposed to do?"

"Improvise."

The man stared at Gran as if she had two heads.

"Isn't that what the greats do? I've seen those cooking shows where they offer the best chefs one ingredient, and they have to make something wonderful around that ingredient. Do that."

He was about to speak but then paused. Stared at her. Then he nodded. "That's another way of looking at it. See what I have and create specials accordingly."

"If meat's scarce, use less of it. If the veggies are a little soft, caramelize them. If the lettuce is old, serve wilted lettuce salad."

"Where is Philip?" asked Riley.

The two cooks shrugged. "We've got no idea," said the second one. "He didn't answer his phone. He was in a dither last night over just about everything, and this morning he didn't show up."

Gran touched Riley's arm.

She looked worried. He couldn't deny that he felt the same way. She headed for the door. "We'll see if we can track him down."

Once in the car, Riley turned her way. "And how exactly are we supposed to track him down?" he asked.

She already had her phone out and was scrolling through her contacts. "His sister Gwen. She and Philip put that phone-find thing on their phones because they're not young and don't have another living soul related to them, so it's a way of knowing what the other's doing if they don't talk. Gwen?" She redirected her attention to the phone, and in less than a minute, Philip's sister had pinpointed his location.

He was across the river in Rockland County.

Riley headed for the beautiful three-mile bridge that linked the two counties. It was less than thirty minutes to the spot on Gwen's phone. And while traffic heading into Sleepy Hollow was heavy, the westbound lanes were lighter and moving quickly.

Twenty-five minutes later, Riley drove into a graveled parking lot.

"That's Philip's old Chrysler, right there," declared Gran. "And there's the old thief himself, coming down those steps."

Riley parked his vehicle perpendicular to Philip's. Philip's car was now blocked by a hill in one direction and Riley's SUV in another.

Riley got out.

So did Gran, just as Tess's car pulled up.

Philip stared at Gran, then Tess, then Riley...

And then he burst into tears.

Chapter Fourteen

Tess read Gran's text eagerly that morning. She and Marita had done hours of prep, and when Riley's mother came by with an offer to help, they'd welcomed her with open arms.

"'Heading to intercept Philip across the river,'" read Tess. "'Send up a prayer or two. We could sure use it.'" Gran had added the address to a place in Rockland County.

Marita pointed to the back door. "I'm a big fan of prayer in action," she told Tess. "You head over there before the roads are totally clogged with tourist traffic. I'll help train our new counter gal," she teased.

Riley's mom turned and aimed a smile their way. She filled trays with breads while Marita warmed soups and Sonya arranged ingredients for Sunday's offerings.

"You're never too old to learn new tricks," Kathy declared. "If I'm going to run the marina, I need something to keep me busy during the off-season. What's better than soup all winter?"

Tess laughed, ditched her apron, and hurried to the door. "Nothing that I can think of." The town roads weren't too bad yet. Once she got to the bridge, it was clear sailing. She knew Riley would keep Gran safe, but the thought of Gran facing off with anyone on top of last week's health scare was concerning. Gran's daughter couldn't be bothered looking out for her own mother, and that was sad.

But Tess could do it happily, and that made a huge difference in both their lives.

She entered the parking lot of an animal sanctuary, pulled up alongside Philip's car, and got out. Philip Rossiter was on the steps, coming down. He looked awful.

Gran turned her way, surprised and maybe a little worried about who was watching over the shop.

Not Riley. He exchanged a look with her that said he understood.

Gran moved forward.

Philip sat down on the steps that led to a wooden arch at the top. He put his head in his hands. Tess didn't know him well, and didn't like what he'd done, but she couldn't help being moved by his despair.

Gran didn't berate. Didn't scold. Didn't yell.

Nope, she took a seat right next to him, handed him a clutch of tissues from her purse, and waited.

"I shouldn't have done it!" He hiccupped the words around emotion, then swiped the wad of tissues to his face.

"Why did you, Philip? I saw the restaurant wasn't kept up the same," she told him. "Riley and I went there this morning, so I saw it firsthand, but to steal money to get Maison Philipe back on its feet—"

"I would never do that!" He stared at her in amazement. "I love my place, but I would never steal from friends for a building."

"Then why?" asked Riley. "I don't understand."

"Pierre."

"The dog?" asked Tess. "Your little dog?"

Tears leaked from his eyes again. "He needed surgery for a problem in his intestines, something the vet said could be fixed. If it wasn't fixed, it would kill him. I told them to go ahead and do the surgery, but then there was a problem and Pierre was put in ICU. I didn't have the money for the surgery, much less an expensive recovery. And I didn't have any credit left. I sank everything into the restaurant to keep up payroll, payments, and supplies, but for the past two years it's been like trying to stop water from running downhill. The money just keeps going out and out and out."

He didn't seem to be overstating the facts. A lot of businesses had suffered in the past couple of years. He was clearly desperate to save the dog and his livelihood. "I was hoping this busy season would fix it, and I would pay all that money back, but even with all the tourists we've had, very few are coming up the hill for fine dining. Not with so many more affordable places in town and along the river now."

"That's one of the fallouts from new development sometimes," said Riley. "It creates more competition than the market can bear."

"I didn't know what to do, but then I saw a fundraiser for needy dogs and cats. I said to myself that my Pierre is a poor little dog with great need, so I created All Creatures. But then so many people gave so much that I got nervous. Scared." He raised red-rimmed eyes to the three of them. "I didn't mean to steal a bunch of money. I only wanted enough to take care of Pierre's bill, but it was like a wildfire of donations. I panicked, so I took everything down and made it go away, but then you got sick and almost died..." He aimed this last at Gran.

"I was nowhere near death, but it was scary," she agreed.

"I didn't know what to do." He redirected his attention to Tess and Riley. "You were both looking for answers, June suffered heart failure because of my actions, and I was trapped."

"So you thought starting a dumpster fire would be a good thing to do?" Tess was surprised Riley could keep the sarcasm out of his voice.

"It wasn't me," Philip protested. "I heard about it and was afraid you would figure this out and blame me, but I would never do such a thing that might hurt others. Or scare them. I just wanted Pierre to be okay. Today I brought the rest of the money here." He pointed up the hill. "To this shelter. I gave it to them, all but the ten thousand it cost for Pierre's medical bills. Somehow, some way I'll pay it back, June. I promise."

Gran met his gaze.

Then she looked up at Riley and Tess. Tess moved forward. "Mr. Rossiter, you said that people aren't coming up the hill for French cuisine, right?"

He nodded, glum.

"What if you rebrand the restaurant?" she suggested.

"Golden arches?" The thought of fast food put genuine angst in his gaze.

She shook her head. "Crepes."

He frowned.

"Crepes are French cuisine, they can be savory or sweet, breakfast, lunch, or dinner. They're very popular all over Manhattan right now and quite affordable. And easily made and adjusted."

She could see she'd sparked his interest about halfway through her spiel.

"They are a coming thing, aren't they?"

"They're all the rage. Good, simple food that doesn't break the bank. And for the high-end people, you could offer a steak-and-mushroom variety with cream sauce."

"A stroganoff!"

Tess nodded.

He swiped his eyes again. "I know I'll have to pay for what I've done. But when it's all over, I'll take this idea and run with it, because this is something I could do and make folks happy. Why didn't I think of it myself?"

"Because you let desperation take hold, Philip," said Gran. "Somewhere along the way you forgot that there's always an honest way out of our troubles." She stood up. "Thank you for donating the rest of the money. That's exactly what it was meant for, and I'm glad you made that move. Now I've got a kitchen to run…"

"You've got a house to go to," Tess corrected her. "I'll be at the shop with our newest employee, Kathy O'Toole. She showed up this morning looking for a job, and I hired her on the spot. She's going to be winter help when the marina's closed."

"My mother came looking for a job?" Now it was Riley's turn to be surprised. "Really?"

"She's filling bread bags even as we speak. Said as long as she was staying in town to run the marina, she wanted to be busy all winter, and what better way to keep busy than to help bake bread and make soup."

She expected his smile because she knew he was worried about his mother's grief and her choices.

What she didn't expect was to have him lift her off the ground, spin her around, and kiss her. Right there in front of Gran and Philip and whoever might be watching from the animal sanctuary.

And she kissed him back.

Chapter Fifteen

It didn't matter that the sun had been shining on a bright October day from the get-go.

The clouds in Riley's brain cleared the minute Tess talked about his mother coming to the soup shop in search of a winter job.

She was staying. Not selling.

That was huge.

The town and the surrounding hills had enjoyed a record-breaking weekend. A crazy number of people streamed in from multiple directions. The smart ones had come in Thursday and seen some of the fall sights on Friday before the crush, and it was good to see so many people exploring mansions, streets, eateries, churches, and of course, the Sleepy Hollow Cemetery.

Gran had invited the donors to a meeting of the minds on Monday night. The group intended to help Philip Rossiter right his wrong with no jail time involved. It seemed the thought of free crepes soothed a lot of ruffled feathers.

Riley was intent on getting to Gran's, but as he turned off Broadway, there was Susan Mary, walking her little goldendoodle. He pulled over to the curb and rolled down his window. "That's a mighty cute little friend you have there, Ms. Andreas."

She flushed, but she moved closer to the car. "After all the fuss I made, I still couldn't resist her when a friend messaged me last week.

This little gal's owner had to go to assisted living and she was bound for a shelter. I just couldn't let that happen. I took one look at that face and it was like God was telling me to open a door. A new one. My husband left a while back and it's been just me, doing everything by myself. Now it's not."

He knew how lonely that could get, but one look at Susan Mary's face said she wasn't lonely anymore. "She's a beauty. And lucky to have you."

"We're lucky to have each other," she replied. "You have a good night now."

"I will." He drove on, smiling.

The town was looking into how to help Derrick VanOrden with his access problem. It might not prevent people from messing up parking during the busy fall season, but they should be able to come up with dedicated space for the army veteran. That was the least they could do.

His mother had decided to stay in Sleepy Hollow for the time being. "If I decide to sell in the future, I know what the market is, but frankly, I don't need that sale to live, and your dad loved this place. I do too. So I'll stay right here," she'd told him and Carrie the night before. She directed the next words at Carrie. "And if you and Doug have to move away, I'll come visit during the off-season."

And now he was here. On Gran's street. About to see Tess again.

There were nine cars parked along the road, but at least this time they all stayed on one side like they were supposed to.

He parked around the corner and walked toward Gran's, but he'd only made it a few feet when he spotted Tess coming his way.

He quickened his step.

So did she. And when he reached her, he grabbed her up into another big hug, the kind that a smart man never wanted to end. "Hey."

"Hey yourself. Am I the only one who feels a little weird that we're not scouting out corners, looking for bad guys anymore?"

"Weird, but nice," he replied. "Not hiding in the bushes gives a man time for other pursuits."

She leaned back in his arms and met his gaze. "Such as?"

"Hanging out with his best girl."

She frowned. "There are others?"

He burst out laughing and hugged her again. "None," he promised, his lips against her ear. "None but you, Tess. And I'd kind of like to keep it that way."

"I know." She laid her head on his chest. "I know. But you'll head back to Rochester, and I'll be here with Gran. I can't leave her, Riley. No, I *could*," she corrected herself. "But I won't."

"You know the good thing about being an IT expert?"

"I'm sure the list is long and varied."

He chuckled. "The good thing is that when you're really good at what you do, and a competitor offers you four times the salary to move to Florida and take over their operations—"

"You're going to Florida?" Oh, the look of surprise on her face was priceless. "Are you kidding me, O'Toole?"

He'd love to tease her, but he'd rather be kissing her, so he cleared the matter up quickly. "I said they *offered* me the job. I didn't say I'd take it, but I did send the deal memo to my bosses at Centurion, and they countered nicely. They also agreed that I could work remotely as long as I was open to three days of in-person per month in Rochester."

"You're staying?" She cupped his face with her hands. Chilly hands right now because temperatures fell quickly with the early-setting sun. "Don't toy with me, Riley."

"Staying. And what would you say to me buying Gran's house, Tess?"

She frowned. "Gran's house isn't up for sale."

"The walk to the restaurant is hard for her. We've got a lot of hills here."

Still frowning. "You're serious."

"This is a great house and a great location. Access to the park, the train, the RiverWalk, and the promenade. The kind of place where you could raise a family someday. Gran told me this morning that the tenants are moving out in January. They're being transferred, so the upstairs apartment will be available. She'll be right there, living above the Sleepy Hollow Soup Shop."

"She's really interested in selling the house?" Tess frowned, pensive. "She's never mentioned such a thing to me, Riley. Ever."

"Because this was the only place you could come home to. Your mom made a new home, and Bridget has her own life. Gran said she needed to keep this house so that if you ever wanted to come home, you could. She wants to move."

"But if you're buying it…"

"Did I say *me*?"

The line between her eyes etched deeper. "You did."

"I meant us, Tess."

Her mouth opened wide. So did those pretty brown eyes. "Riley."

"Tess, there's no sense fighting it. We were meant to be together. Everyone says so, so it must be true," he teased.

She studied him. His eyes, his face, his lips...

And then she kissed him.

Really kissed him.

When she was done kissing him, she leaned back in his arms once more. "Is this the O'Toole version of a proposal?"

"Pretty much," he teased. "But I can make it more proper. As long as you say yes." He dropped to one knee, the good one that hadn't gotten messed up with high school and college sports, and held out the ring he'd purchased that morning. "Will you marry me, Tess? Hang out here with the orange-and-black street signs, the traffic, and the crazy winds that come off the river? Forever?"

She kissed him again. And then again. And when he stood and took her in his arms again, she said one simple word. "Yes."

He put the ring on her finger.

It fit, but that was because Gran had given him one of Tess's rings for sizing. It was convenient to have the girl's family on your side. Then he drew her in against his chest. His heart.

He'd come back to Sleepy Hollow to bury his father. He'd stayed to help his mother. And now he'd be here to take that next wonderful step, to start a home and a family with Tess.

Who could ask for anything more?

He wrapped an arm around her as they started for the house. "You do like kids, don't you?"

She laughed. "What if I said no? That's the kind of conversation you have *before* you offer the ring, O'Toole. And yes. I love 'em. I'm always a little sad that Bridget's are so far away. And I'm a big-family kind of gal, Riley. Just so you know."

A big family? With Tess and all the chaos that would entail?

in Sleepy Hollow, New York

He squeezed her shoulder lightly as they went up the steps to the front porch. "Happy to do my part, sweetheart."

She laughed up at him.

He smiled down at her, and then they went through the door just the way they should.

Together.

Dear Friend,

When I first heard the title, *Love's a Mystery*, my mind went to the most mysterious place I know, Sleepy Hollow, home of the famous story, "The Legend of Sleepy Hollow." I had always wondered what became of the story's characters, Brom and Katrina. Did they live happily ever after? *Love Learns the Truth* is the result of my romantic musings.

I created their only daughter, Hannie, to be the heroine of my story. Then I added a handsome new schoolmaster, Gideon, who is the opposite of Ichabod Crane—and Hannie's perfect match, though it takes a bit of convincing for both of them.

Finally, I turned it into a mystery as a stranger comes to town accusing Brom of murdering Ichabod. In solving the mystery of what really happened to him, Hannie and Gideon discover a love neither one saw coming.

My hope is you too will be swept away into a mysterious setting, rich with folklore and romance, and see the hand of God working through these unforgettable characters.

Fondly,
Gabrielle

Dear Fellow Romantic,

Recently, I took a road trip to Sleepy Hollow wondering what would draw my character, Tess, back to her hometown. I enjoyed walking the streets of this lovely, quaint town. Small businesses, just like Sleepy Hollow Soup Shop are everywhere and the old Hudson Valley churches are beautiful. The history and magic of the place lives on every corner.

It was the perfect place to set my mystery of who stole Gran's and her friends' money. Introducing Tess's high school crush, Riley, back into her life at such a vulnerable moment made for a fun, romantic mystery.

I hope you will enjoy. *Love Stirs the Pot* was a pleasure to write. You'll love how the past treads on the heels of the present and sets the stage for something poignant and wonderful. As a mom and now a grandma, I've come to realize that home is where the heart is… and I wanted Tess to know that too. Enjoy my timeless story of love, mystery, and second chances.

Warmly,
Ruthy

About the Authors

Gabrielle Meyer

Gabrielle Meyer lives on the banks of the upper Mississippi River in central Minnesota with her husband and four children. As an employee of the Minnesota Historical Society, she fell in love with history and enjoys writing historical, contemporary, and cozy mystery novels inspired by the past. When Gabrielle is not writing, you might find her homeschooling her children, cheering them on at sporting and theatrical events, or hosting a gathering at her home with family and friends. You can learn more by visiting her at GabrielleMeyer.com or by finding her at Facebook.com/Author GabrielleMeyer, where she spends far too much time.

Ruth Logan Herne

Multipublished, bestselling, and award-winning author Ruth Logan Herne is living her dream of writing and publishing novels, running a farm, telling fourteen grandkids "No!" and "Stop that!" (a favorite line from *Steel Magnolias*), baking for her farm market, fixing things that break, and watching brilliant athletes perform on local Little

League and soccer fields. An avid baker, Ruthy has worn many hats, hairnets, and name tags in her multitude of jobs over the years, but she's pretty sure that just makes her stories more real!

Friend her on Facebook, check out her website ruthloganherne.com, and feel free to email Ruthy at loganherne@gmail.com.

Story Behind the Name

Sleepy Hollow, New York

Perhaps no town in America conjures up such an immediately recognizable image: a dark-clad horseman with a pumpkin for a head, galloping through streets and cemeteries at breakneck speed into the night. The story of Brom Bones and Ichabod Crane and the fair Katrina Van Tassel were made legendary by author Washington Irving, who published the tale in his collection of essays and short stories, *Sketch Book of Geoffrey Crayon, Gent*, in 1820.

But the name goes back much further than Irving's account. In 1655, Dutch settler Adriaen Van der Donk wrote of an idyllic place called *Slapershaven*, which translates into English as Sleeper's Haven, which eventually became Sleepy Hollow, an area inside North Tarrytown. By the early 1700s, Sleepy Hollow was bustling with mills, where farmers from the area brought their grain to be ground, and families came to worship at the beautiful stone Dutch Reformed church and bury their dead in the Old Dutch Burying Ground.

Today, the entire village of North Tarrytown has been officially renamed Sleepy Hollow. Twenty-five miles north of New York City, the area attracts visitors from far and wide who are drawn to the region's stunning rivers, streams, mountains, wooded trails, and of course the shops and eateries. The oldest church building in New York State, the 1697 Dutch Reformed Church still stands watch over this legendary place.

Hannie's Beef & Barley Soup

Ingredients:

2 tablespoons olive oil

1 medium yellow onion, chopped

2 tablespoons minced garlic

1 stalk celery, chopped

2 carrots, chopped

1 small green pepper, diced

1–2 pounds charred (but not burned) bite-sized beef strips

6 cups beef broth

1 large fresh tomato or 1 (15 ounce) can diced tomatoes, undrained

2/3 cup barley

1 tablespoon Worcestershire sauce

1/4 teaspoon dried thyme

1 cup beef gravy made from drippings of the cooked beef

1 bay leaf

2 tablespoons fresh parsley

2 tablespoons red wine (optional)

salt & pepper to taste

Instructions:

Cook onion, garlic, celery, and carrots in olive oil over medium heat until soft. Add remaining ingredients and bring to a boil. Reduce heat. Simmer, covered, about 45 minutes or until barley is tender. Remove bay leaf. Serve. (If needed, add extra broth to reach desired consistency.) Serves eight.

Read on for a sneak peek of another exciting book in the Love's a Mystery series!

Love's a Mystery *in* CAPE DISAPPOINTMENT, WASHINGTON

by LESLIE GOULD & LISA LUDWIG

Love's Beacon
By Leslie Gould

Cape Disappointment, Washington
Friday, February 3, 1899

Sitting on her steamer trunk, Julia Warren looked past the wharf to the mighty Columbia River, blaming it for her wobbly knees. It had only been a two-hour boat ride from Astoria, but it felt as if it had been two days.

She seemed to have lost her childhood sea legs, but at least she still had her stomach of steel. She'd never suffered from seasickness in her life—and planned not to, not even in the location deemed the "Graveyard of the Pacific."

The midafternoon sun shone brightly in the clear blue sky. Wind off the river tugged at her curls under her securely pinned hat, but the relentless Northwest rain Uncle Edward had written about was nowhere to be seen.

She turned toward the town of Ilwaco, really no more than a village. Beyond the wharf and cluster of canneries were houses and businesses. A train ran from the docks into the town and, Julia knew from Uncle Edward's letters, on up the Long Beach Peninsula. Evergreen trees covered the hill, most likely Cape Disappointment. She couldn't see the lighthouse, where Uncle Edward was the keeper, from where she stood. But she knew it was up there. Somewhere.

She squinted into the afternoon sun. Clouds formed over the hill. Perhaps the sunny day would be short lived. What kind of bird flew above the cape? A boy on the wharf pointed to it. "Look at the eagle, Ma!" he called out to the woman next to him.

"It looks just like the one we saw this morning." His mother took his hand and hurried toward town.

Perhaps it was unusual to see eagles in this far southwestern corner of Washington State. Regardless, it was unusual for Julia. Occasionally, she'd see an eagle on the outskirts of Philadelphia, but not often. She pivoted around to face the street off the wharf. She'd sent Uncle Edward a telegram from Denver, saying she'd probably be a day later than she expected due to blizzards slowing down the train. But then she'd made her connection in Portland after all. Was he here to meet her on the chance that she'd made it on time? She scanned the crowd of people for her uncle but saw no one with a white beard and hair. No worries. She was sure she could find a driver to take her to the lighthouse.

And on the way, she'd stop by the office of the Ilwaco newspaper. She'd lived frugally in Philadelphia and saved what she could, but living expenses took most of her salary. Then, when she was in Denver, a packet of her money went missing from her bag, most likely taken as she dozed in the train station. She had wanted to find a job out west if she could, but now it was imperative that she did so soon. She didn't want to be dependent on Uncle Edward.

Surely, with a degree from Vassar and seven years of experience at the *Philadelphia Times*, she'd qualify to work as a reporter for a village newspaper.

However, after her disastrous relationship with Jack Turner, she wouldn't grow close to a newspaperman, ever again. Jack had taught her everything she knew about the business—and then he broke her heart. She wouldn't let it happen again.

"Need a ride, miss?" A young man wearing a brown coat and a derby hat nodded to a buggy on the street. He had a kind smile and a handsome face. "I can take you anywhere within a few miles. My name is Billy Jones. Everyone knows me here."

"Perfect." Julia grabbed her own hat as a gust of wind whipped against the blue felt as if it were a sail. Perhaps it wasn't secured as tightly as she thought. "I need to stop by the newspaper office while I am here in town. Then, my destination is the lighthouse." She stepped away from her trunk.

"All right." Billy lifted the trunk. "Is Alexander Blake expecting you?"

"I don't know that name."

"He's the owner of the *Cape Dispatch*."

She smiled. "He isn't expecting me. I wanted to speak to someone about a position. Perhaps the publisher or editor would be more inclined to have a spare moment."

"Miss, he's the publisher and editor, along with being the owner."

"I see."

"And the main reporter."

"Well." She stepped quickly to keep up with the driver. "That settles it." She brushed her hands together. "Take me to Mr. Alexander Blake, please."

They passed the Ilwaco Railway train depot, and then Billy stopped in front of a wooden building on Main Street. He jumped down and gave her a hand.

"The office for the *Dispatch* is on the right side of the building. There's a side door." He nodded to the alley between the large white building and a small brick one. The large building had the words WINTHER'S GENERAL STORE painted above the door.

Julia stepped onto the boardwalk and then around the side of the building into the alley. She stepped purposefully around several puddles—obviously it had rained recently—not wanting to muddy her button-up boots. When she reached the side door, she turned the knob and walked in.

A large desk, covered with papers, sat in the middle of the room with a chair behind it. A large table was pushed against the wall.

"Hello!" Julia called out.

When no one responded, she called a little louder. "Mr. Blake? Are you on the premises?"

She started toward the closed door on the interior wall as it was flung open. A man nearly a head taller than Julia with broad shoulders, thick dark hair, and lively brown eyes greeted her. "Good afternoon. How may I help you?"

Julia groaned within at the sight of another handsome newspaper man. At least this time, she'd know to guard herself. "I am Julia Warren, recently employed as a reporter with the *Philadelphia Times*. I'm inquiring about a position as a reporter."

He extended his hand, then noticed the ink stains and swiped his hand down his apron as he nodded in greeting instead. "Alexander Blake. Pleased to meet you. Any chance you know how to set type?"

She took a step backward. "No." That was one thing she hadn't learned in Philadelphia.

He sighed. "That's a shame." He led her through the door into the next room.

Inside, reams of paper lined the floor next to a printing press. Mr. Blake started to say something to the man standing beside the press, but a bell from the street began to clang.

Mr. Blake took off his apron and tossed it behind him. "Finish setting the last article and then start running the press," he said to the other man. "The delivery boys will be here soon." Then he stepped past Julia, saying, "Excuse me," as he did and headed toward the door, where he grabbed an oilcloth coat from the rack.

"Come on," he said to her. "I'm closing shop."

"Don't you have a newspaper to print?"

"It'll get done, one way or the other. It always does." He opened the door and then wiggled into his coat. "I'm in a hurry."

"Goodness." Jack had been a scoundrel but never this rude.

As Julia stepped out into the alley, Mr. Blake bounded through the door after her. Trying to get out of his way and not step in a puddle, she dodged to the right at the same time he did. They collided, and she feared the impact would topple her. But he quickly grabbed her elbow. "My apologies," he said. "I certainly didn't mean to send you tumbling."

She planted her feet and steadied herself. "I'm quite all right."

"Are you sure?"

She nodded.

"I'm sorry," he said. "I got ahead of myself. I can't afford a reporter at this time, but let's talk later. Perhaps on Monday?"

"All right."

The clanging of the bell grew louder. She started toward the street and the buggy. Mr. Blake rushed past her.

Someone shouted. "It's a sailboat, taking on water. The tide is washing it up to the beach."

As she rounded the corner, Mr. Blake was yelling at her driver. "Billy, are you coming?"

Billy hopped down from the buggy. "Maybe later. I'm giving this lady a ride to the lighthouse. I'll stop by on my way back."

As Julia reached the buggy, a man stepped from the boardwalk and offered her his hand. He had blond hair, blue eyes, and a charming smile. Were all the men in these parts so handsome?

As she took his hand and climbed into the buggy, the man said, "I'm Lucien Graham. Welcome to Ilwaco." He gestured to Mr. Blake. "Don't mind our newspaper man. He's always in a hurry."

She smiled. "I'm Julia Warren. From Philadelphia."

"Ahh, Edward Warren's niece?" he said.

She nodded.

"Isn't he expecting you tomorrow?"

"He is," she answered. "But I was able to make my original connection in Portland."

"I'm an assistant lightkeeper on the cape," Mr. Graham said. "Mr. Warren is working tonight. He'd want you to go straight to the lighthouse."

"Thank you." She glanced back at the general store. "Perhaps I should place a telephone call first, to let Uncle Edward know I'll be arriving soon."

Mr. Graham laughed, his voice booming. "You just gave yourself away as a big-city girl. The telephone hasn't made its way to Ilwaco yet. Astoria is the nearest, so far. We're hoping it will arrive here within the decade."

"Oh," Julia said. Nearly every business and many of the homes in Philadelphia, even the boardinghouse she lived in, had telephones. It hadn't occurred to her that Cape Disappointment wouldn't.

As Billy approached the buggy, Mr. Graham said something to him. Billy nodded and then jumped up into the driver's seat. As the buggy began to roll, Julia said, "I take it Mr. Blake is off to report on the sailboat that's sinking."

"Yes, ma'am," Billy said. "And to help save the crew. He's part of the volunteer rescue brigade."

The forest grew dense on the edge of town and as Billy drove the horse up the plank road, Julia pulled her coat tight. The damp chill in the air, even though it wasn't raining, began to seep into her bones. Through breaks in the trees, she could see clouds billowing over the Pacific, although she didn't have a view of the ocean yet. She expected the rain wouldn't hold off for long.

The light grew dimmer as the trees grew thicker. Finally, the road crested, and two houses appeared.

"Those are the keepers' houses," Billy said.

"They're lovely." Life on Cape Disappointment would be more comfortable than she'd expected. "But where's the lighthouse?"

"Around the corner."

"Can you take me there?"

"Yes, ma'am. Do you want to drop off your trunk first?"

"No, we can do that on the way back." At home in Rhode Island, the keeper's residence had been on the ground floor of the lighthouse, not "around the corner."

When they reached the lighthouse, it was clear that daylight was waning. Julia scrambled down from the buggy before Billy could help her, raised her skirts, ran to the lighthouse, and flung open the door.

"Uncle Edward," she called out. "I'm here!"

"What in the world?" came a husky voice from above.

She hurried to the staircase and started up. But coming down was a man much younger than Uncle Edward.

"You must be looking for Mr. Warren?"

Julia froze, clutching the handrailing. "Yes. Where is he?"

"He's at the Cape Disappointment Lighthouse."

"Isn't this the Cape Disappointment Lighthouse?"

He shook his head. "This is the North Head Lighthouse on Cape Disappointment. I'm John Parker. The keeper here."

"Oh." Uncle Edward hadn't mentioned there were two lighthouses on the cape.

"It's only a short distance away. Two miles or so."

"All right," Julia said, backing down the stairs. "Thank you."

When she reached the buggy, she told Billy about the mix-up.

"I'm sorry, ma'am. I thought you meant this lighthouse."

"No." She hoped she hid her disappointment. "I'm the niece of Edward Warren, the keeper of the Cape Disappointment lighthouse." She couldn't blame Billy. "I'm sorry. It's not your fault."

The first drops of rain were soft against her hands. But then the wind picked up and the rain began to sting her face. Now an iciness settled deep inside her, colder than the blizzard in Denver.

A few minutes later, darkness fell completely. Billy stopped and lit a lantern and then hung it on the buggy. "It's not much farther," he said. "See." He pointed. "You can see the beacon."

The beam of light flashed.

The lighthouse—and Uncle Edward—weren't far now.

***

Soon the road turned, and the beacon was out of sight. Julia buried her hands in her coat and tried to ignore the icy rain. She'd soon be in the lighthouse, brewing a cup of tea and telling Uncle Edward about her trip. She smiled at the thought, but then a shout startled her out of her daze.

"It must be the rescuers on the beach," Billy said. "By now they should have any survivors from the sailboat on the shore."

A bell began to clang again—whether it was the same one as before, she didn't know, although this one was more distant, and there were more shouts.

"It's the *Pacific Star*," someone yelled. "It's on the bar."

"Whoa." Billy brought the horse to a stop. "That's much more serious than the sailboat sinking. I need to go down to the beach, to see if they need me to go for help or anything. There's a trail here." He grabbed the lantern. "I'll be right back."

Julia wasn't staying by herself. "I'm going with you." She scrambled down from the bench.

Billy led the way to the trail. "It's steep." He held the lantern up high as he sidestepped down the trail. "Watch out for the tree roots," he said to Julia. And then, "There's a rock here. Don't step on it—it's slick."

The wind snatched at her hat again and Julia held on to it. Until she slipped. Her feet flew out from under her, slamming into Billy and causing the lantern to go flying. Both of them fell, sliding down the trail. Finally, Billy grabbed a branch, stopping both of them.

"I'm sorry," she said.

"Are you all right?" he asked.

"I'm fine." At least she hoped she was.

"Can you stand?"

"Yes."

He helped her up then scrambled back up the hill for the lantern. The flame had gone out, but he took matches from his coat pocket and relit it. Then he returned, holding the lantern high once again. Julia wiped her muddy gloved hands on her equally muddy skirt.

"We need to send out the rescue boat!" someone yelled.

"Let's go," Billy said, taking her hand. "The trail is easier from here."

When the trail flattened, Billy let go of her hand. A dozen lanterns lit up the beach, showing a rescue boat with a rope attached to a wooden cart at the edge of the water. Several men shoved the boat into the waves.

Beyond, a lifeboat bobbed in the ocean and, past it, the waves battered a ship.

"Billy!" Mr. Blake approached. "You missed going out on the rescue boat."

"I only came down to see if you needed me to go get more help."

Mr. Blake's eyes met Julia's. "I didn't expect to see you again so soon."

"Billy is driving me to the lighthouse."

Billy motioned to the ship. "What's going on with the *Pacific Star*?"

"It's stuck on the bar. The men are going to try to pull it off with the rope, if it's long enough to reach. I think the ship may be too big though, even if it is."

A man in a bowler hat approached them. "Is that really the *Pacific Star*?" It appeared he'd run to the beach.

"That's right, Mr. Petersen," Alexander said. "It's stuck on the bar."

"It's being rescued, right?"

"We don't know yet." Alexander spoke kindly to the man. "Hopefully."

"It's breaking up!" someone on the rescue boat shouted.

Another lifeboat appeared, coming from the ship.

"We need to get the cargo!" Mr. Petersen shouted.

"We need to save the lives!" someone from the rescue boat shouted back.

Julia wondered if Uncle Edward could see from the lighthouse what was happening. She glanced up to the bluff and waited, but the beacon wasn't in view.

Fog began to roll in from the ocean, and she directed her attention to the disappearing boats until Mr. Blake pointed at the bluff. "The beacon is out."

"You should be able to see it from here?" Julia asked.

"Yes," Mr. Blake replied. "It was lit. But it's out now."

Julia swallowed hard. Something must have happened.

"What's going on?"

A man came bounding onto the beach from the trail. *Mr. Graham.*

"It's the *Pacific Star*," Billy called out. "Stuck on the bar."

"And the beacon is out." Mr. Blake pointed to the bluff again.

Mr. Graham turned. "It was on a little while ago—I saw it when I came from town." He started back to the trail. "Something must have happened. Mr. Warren wouldn't let the beacon go out."

A Note from the Editors

We hope you enjoyed the first volume in the Love's a Mystery series, published by Guideposts. For over seventy-five years Guideposts, a nonprofit organization, has been driven by a vision of a world filled with hope. We aspire to be the voice of a trusted friend, a friend who makes you feel more hopeful and connected.

By making a purchase from Guideposts, you join our community in touching millions of lives, inspiring them to believe that all things are possible through faith, hope, and prayer. Your continued support allows us to provide uplifting resources to those in need. Whether through our online communities, websites, apps, or publications, we strive to inspire our audiences, bring them together, comfort, uplift, entertain, and guide them.

To learn more, please go to guideposts.org.

Find more inspiring stories in these best-loved Guideposts fiction series!

Mysteries of Lancaster County
Follow the Classen sisters as they unravel clues and uncover hidden secrets in Mysteries of Lancaster County. As you get to know these women and their friends, you'll see how God brings each of them together for a fresh start in life.

Secrets of Wayfarers Inn
Retired schoolteachers find themselves owners of an old warehouse-turned-inn that is filled with hidden passages, buried secrets, and stunning surprises that will set them on a course to puzzling mysteries from the Underground Railroad.

Tearoom Mysteries Series
Mix one stately Victorian home, a charming lakeside town in Maine, and two adventurous cousins with a passion for tea and hospitality. Add a large scoop of intriguing mystery, and sprinkle generously with faith, family, and friends, and you have the recipe for *Tearoom Mysteries*.

Ordinary Women of the Bible
Richly imagined stories—based on facts from the Bible—have all the plot twists and suspense of a great mystery, while bringing you fascinating insights on what it was like to be a woman living in the ancient world.

To learn more about these books, visit Guideposts.org/Shop